PERSONAL AFFECTS

Volume II

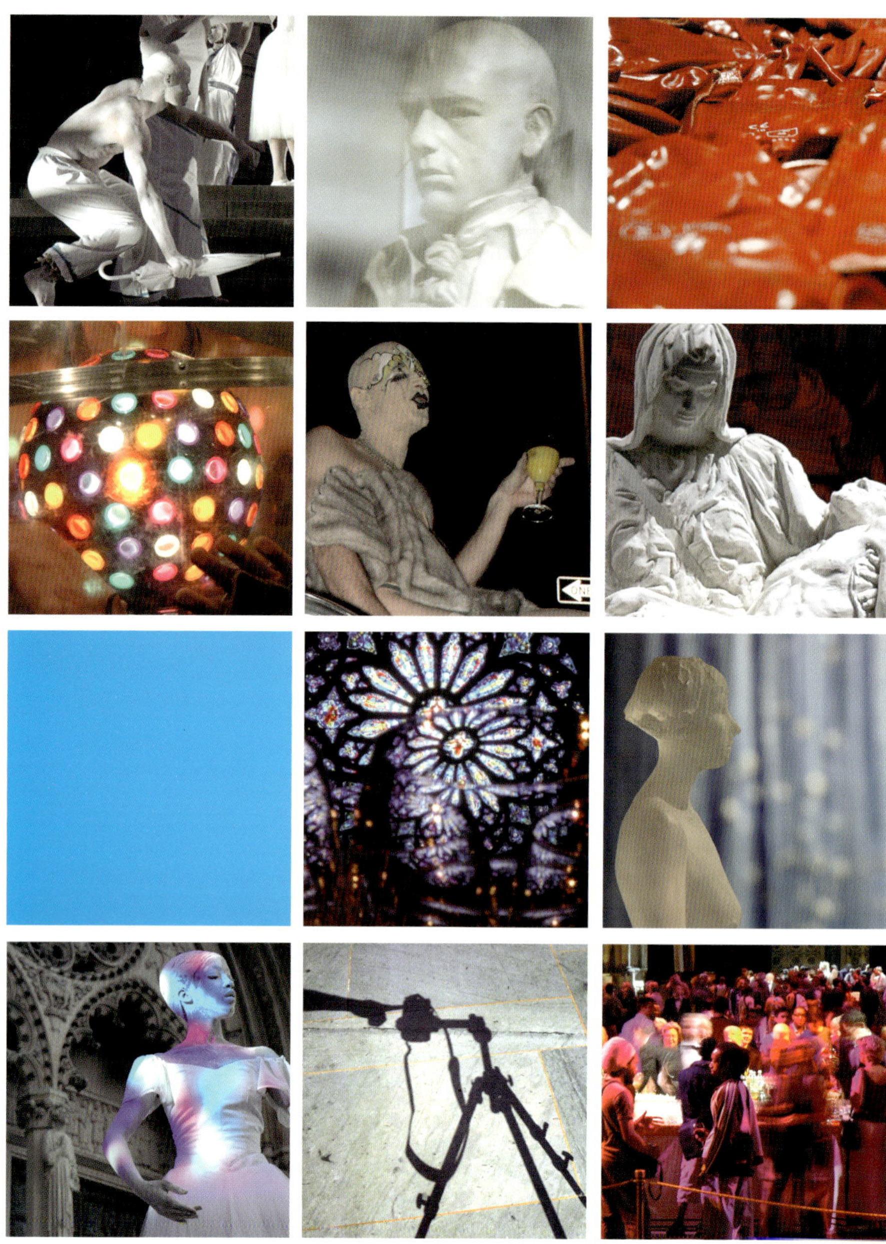

PERSONAL AFFECTS

Power and Poetics in Contemporary South African Art

Volume II

Curated by

David Brodie

Laurie Ann Farrell

Churchill Madikida

Sophie Perryer

Liese van der Watt

With essay by

Steven Nelson

MUSEUM FOR AFRICAN ART New York

SPIER Cape Town

PERSONAL AFFECTS VOLUME II
is published in conjunction with an exhibition
of the same title organized by the
**Museum for African Art, New York
and Spier, Cape Town**

September 21 2004 – January 3 2005

*The exhibition is presented at the Museum for African Art
and the Cathedral of St John the Divine, New York,
as part of Season South Africa*

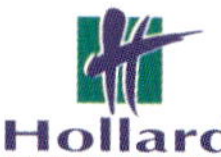

The catalogue is sponsored by Hollard

Season South Africa is sponsored by Spier, Brand South Africa, Nando's,
Hollard, and Winecorp and its Spier Wines.
Additional support for the exhibition has been provided by the
Consulate General of the Netherlands in New York.

Curators

David Brodie, Laurie Ann Farrell, Churchill Madikida, Sophie Perryer, Liese van der Watt

Editor

Sophie Perryer

Available through DAP/Distributed Art Publishers
155 Sixth Avenue, 2nd Floor, New York, NY 10013
Tel: (212) 627-1999 Fax: (212) 627-9484
www.artbook.com

Photography by Mario Todeschini with the exception of pp 62–64 courtesy of Robin Rhode;
p 70 Berni Searle; p 71–73 Laurie Ann Farrell; p 83 and 85 Minnette Vári; p 89 Kathy Grundlingh

*Every effort has been made to trace all copyright holders but if any have
inadvertently been overlooked, the publisher will be pleased to make
the necessary arrangements at the first opportunity.*

Library of Congress Control Number: 2004111257
Paper bound ISBN 0-945802-44-7

Design by Gillian Fraenkel
Reproduction by Hirt and Carter, Cape Town
Printed and bound in Singapore by Tien Wah Press

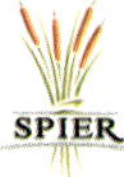 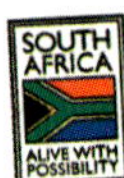 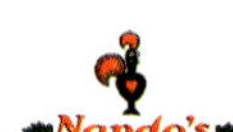 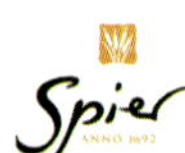 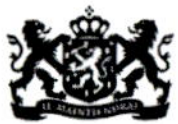

CONTENTS

FOREWORD

I am in awe of the imagination of the 17 participating artists in responding to the spaces of the Cathedral of St John the Divine and the Museum for African Art in New York. The installation of *Personal Affects* at both venues exceeded all my expectations and the openings, particularly the launch of *Season South Africa* at the Cathedral, were truly invigorating and exhilarating evenings.

Images will remain in my mind for years to come of the performance by Jay Pather's company on the steps of the Cathedral, which brought the traffic on Amsterdam Avenue to a halt; of Steven Cohen suspended in the dark, cavernous Nave with his *Chandelier* twinkling above the audience; and of the Cathedral dignitaries beating Samson Mudzunga's drum. There are, equally, many quiet, contemplative installations and projections that continue to resonate for me and, I am sure, for many other people.

I would like to thank the artists without whom there would be no exhibition, the team of curators – David Brodie, Laurie Ann Farrell, Churchill Madikida, Sophie Perryer and Liese van der Watt – and Ralph Freese, Michael Stevenson and Kurt Ackermann for their management of the year-long process that resulted in these exhibitions and performances. We are very grateful to the institutions of the Cathedral of St John the Divine and the Museum for African Art whose staff have been extraordinarily committed to the project and the complex installation process. Thanks are also due to South Africa's Ambassador to the United States, Barbara Masekela, for the inspiring words of her address at the launch of *Season South Africa*.

These exhibitions would have remained mere ideas if it were not for the sponsors who generously supported the project: Brand South Africa, Nando's, and Hollard.

I hope these exhibitions have given South African artists and curators an idea of the stimulus of New York, and that they also give New Yorkers much pleasure and a small insight into our complex and vibrant country.

Dick Enthoven

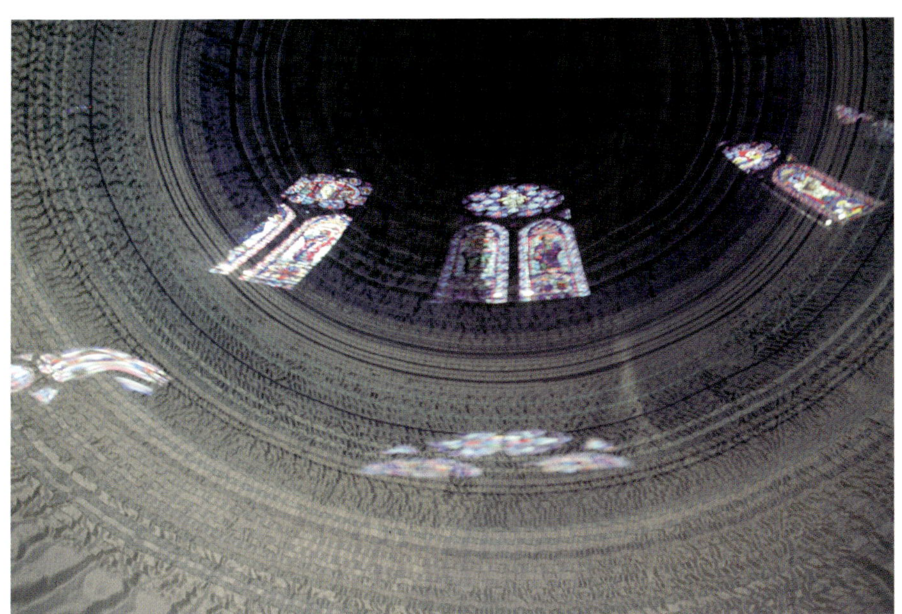

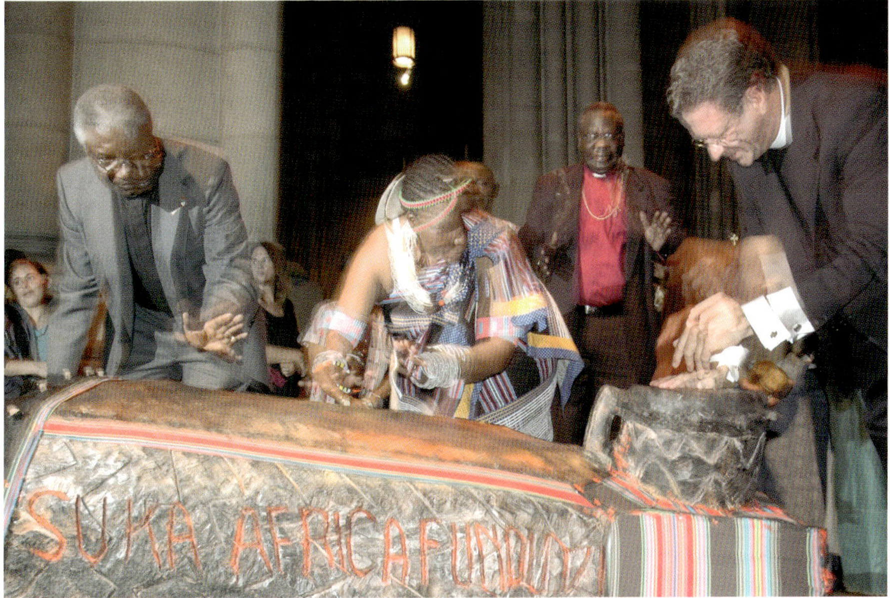
SUKA AFRICAFUNDUZI

INTRODUCTION

The second volume of the catalogue for *Personal Affects: Power and Poetics in Contemporary South African Art* is published in celebration of the exhibition which opened at two venues, the Museum for African Art and the Cathedral of St John the Divine in New York, in September 2004. The first catalogue, in line with curatorial aims for the show, emphasized working processes and the artists' own voices, in the form of interviews around the formulation of the artists' proposals, and documentation of works in progress. This second volume presents the works as they were realized, installed and finally viewed, along with an accompanying essay by American academic Steven Nelson.

The artists, who visited New York in February 2004 to view the spaces before submitting their proposals, returned to the city in September to install their works. This allowed the opportunity for numerous changes and revisions in terms of placement and detail. In the Cathedral in particular, the overwhelming space provided a continual challenge to artists and curators to ensure that works were at once strong enough to stand up to their surroundings, and integrated so as to occupy them harmoniously. Added to this, the Cathedral had recently begun a reconstruction campaign, which simultaneously closed off and created new spaces that could be occupied. The artists' ongoing involvement in the form that the exhibition took again underscored the curatorial intention of foregrounding the artists' personal involvement in the show.

Indeed, installing the work in situ at the Cathedral highlighted process and dialogue emphatically: exhibition design plans had to be reassessed, adjusted and sometimes discarded altogether, and unexpected juxtapositions brought surprising new meanings into works. So for instance, Sandile Zulu put the finishing touches to his installation by sourcing stones from the Hudson river and placing these at key points in the Chapel of St Boniface, emphasizing the centrality of nature and the elements to his artmaking. Mustafa Maluka, working on his tribute to Cape Flats rapper and social activist Mr Devious, disappeared to Chinatown for a day to source bunches of plastic flowers, adding an unplanned but profound detail to his work. Churchill Madikida made an altar for his video, *Blood on My Hands*, with purchased objects including a plaster head of Christ, the Bible and candles. Claudette Schreuders' saint/Mami Wata figure, *The Free Girl,* was only complete once devotional candles and a red velvet kneeling cushion had been placed before her. Thando Mama's 46 figures painted onto glass found resonance in the gold figures decorating the altar in the Chapel of St Ambrose, while Clive van den Berg's *Love's Ballast,* a carved figure reclining on a bier with hands outstretched, found its visual echo two bays down, in the marble memorial to a bishop. Minnette Vári's video installation in the Chapel of St Columba required the construction of a massive screen that obscured the altar, framed along the top by beautiful stained glass windows.

Installation took place simultaneously at the Museum and the Cathedral, with Steven Cohen and his partner Elu practically living in Cohen's *Boudoir,* a room created at the Museum, which gradually filled up with an accumulation of objects to provide a personal setting for the screening of his video, *Chandelier.* Minnette Vári spent days setting the moulded image of her face into a wall, its mouth the peephole through which her video

Cyclops was viewed. One of the most time-consuming feats was the hanging of Wim Botha's *Mnemonic Reconstruction*, an extraordinarily complex suspended room which involved architectural consultations about weight-bearing points in the Museum's ceiling.

The exhibition opened at the Museum on September 21, with performances of choreographer Jay Pather's *Hotel* and performance artist Steven Cohen's *Free Jew is cheap at twice the price*. Enclosed in the plastic bubble of a gumball machine, Cohen used a tiny camera to scrutinize his body and a photograph of Hitler up close, images of which were projected inside *Boudoir*. Two days later spectacular performances again set the tone for the launch of *Season South Africa* and the opening of *Personal Affects* at the Cathedral. Twenty-four dancers choreographed by Jay Pather started the proceedings on the front steps with *From Before*. This was followed by Steven Cohen's descent from the heights of the Nave, dressed as a living, glowing chandelier, and Samson Mudzunga's emergence from inside a massive carved wooden drum in a symbolic enactment of his personal freedom. The drum was then presented as a gift to the people of New York by the South African Ambassador to the United States, Barbara Masekela, who hosted the evening.

The artists' participation extended to a day of panel discussions at the Museum, where many of them provided illuminating personal insights into their artistic practice and answered questions from the audience. There was extensive discussion of the curatorial process, which once again emphasized the artists. Augmented by wall texts featuring quotes by the artists, and with the overall theme and title of the show fully conceptualised only once proposals from artists had been received, it became clear that the realization of *Personal Affects* was very much the result of a collaborative effort between artists and curators.

The curators are thus extremely grateful to the artists for their continued engagement with the processes of the exhibition, their incredible works and their energy throughout the conception and installation process. We would also like to thank again Dick Enthoven for his vision and generosity; Ralph Freese for his wise counsel; Michael Stevenson for his ongoing advice; and project manager Kurt Ackermann for his attention to the myriad details and logistics of these events.

Thanks to the Board of Trustees and staff of the Museum for African Art, including Elsie McCabe, President; Jerome Vogel, Deputy Director; Kenita Lloyd, Director of Operations; Giacomo Mirabella, Registrar; Heidi Holder, Director of Education; Carol Braide, Publications Manager; Margo Donaldson, Senior Development Officer; Michelle Pinedo, Project Accountant; and Lawerence Ekechi, Winston Rodney, Winston M Rodney, and Yensi Martinez, Security. Thanks are also due to the staff of the Cathedral of St John the Divine, to the Rev Canon Tom Miller for his faith in the process, and Ken Williams for his facilitation of the installation at the Cathedral.

David Brodie
Laurie Ann Farrell
Churchill Madikida
Sophie Perryer
Liese van der Watt

POST–SOUTH AFRICA?

Steven Nelson

Personal Affects: Power and Poetics in Contemporary South African Art is an exhibition that encompasses seventeen artists, five curators and two venues. The artists – Jane Alexander, Wim Botha, Steven Cohen, Churchill Madikida, Mustafa Maluka, Thando Mama, Samson Mudzunga, Jay Pather, Johannes Phokela, Robin Rhode, Claudette Schreuders, Berni Searle, Doreen Southwood, Clive van den Berg, Minnette Vári, Diane Victor and Sandile Zulu – were brought to New York to visit the city, the Museum for African Art and the Cathedral of St John the Divine in February 2004, and asked to propose works for the current show. Rarely is there the opportunity to write a catalogue essay for an exhibition consisting of mostly newly commissioned pieces after the work has been completed and installed, but *Personal Affects'* strategy of a two-part catalogue exists as an exception to the rule, allowing for an examination of the visual results of the artists' respective experiences in New York. In the end, sixteen of the artists chose to exhibit in both venues. Robin Rhode chose only to exhibit at the Museum.

Personal Affects is a paradoxical exhibition. On one hand, it begs to be thought of as post- a number of things (a point to which I shall return), and it seeks to be viewed as a site of highly individual artistic achievements. In the first part of the catalogue, the curators – David Brodie, Laurie Ann Farrell, Churchill Madikida, Sophie Perryer and Liese van der Watt – rightly underscore the highly personal nature of the works, asking the viewer, if only indirectly, to see the artists as individuals with complex practices, something we take for granted with artists (at least white ones) from the West.

On the other hand, as part of *Season South Africa,* which commemorates the tenth anniversary of democracy in South Africa, *Personal Affects* presents visual art and artists as ambassadors of goodwill, an attitude underscored by a number of speakers, both South African and American, at the opening festivities at the Cathedral. Under such a rubric, individual achievements read as "South African Art, 2004". Furthermore, South Africa, at least in the art world, is often less a geographic place than a mode of reception. However, if the objects in the Cathedral and at the Museum as well as their creators are ambassadors of goodwill, they are ambivalent ones at best.

In 1995, Rasheed Araeen, in the context of the first Johannesburg Biennale, asked how a newly democratic South Africa would take its place in the international art world. Concerned with difference, inclusion and the residue of the exclusion of South Africa from the international art circuit, as well as the West's obsessive fascination with non-Western cultures, Araeen, reading through David Koloane, saw the possibility that 350 years of colonization and racist oppression would become transformed into what Koloane called "an appropriate aesthetic classification".[1]

What Araeen and Koloane, among others, suggested is that the complexities of South African visual practices, particularly when viewed in the West, would herald a new mode of reception, a mode called "South Africa". Alongside the replacement of "Babel" by "rainbow" in this mode of reception, in the international exhibitions that followed the first Johannesburg Biennale, art from South Africa, as articulation of a politics of identity, as evidence of a politics of struggle, as an archive of suffering experienced by both oppressor and oppressed, became standard fare for a Western audience fascinated with liberation, truth and reconciliation (though not its own), and expressions from a South Africa now simplistically coded as the "rainbow nation". In this process, there was indeed forged a narrow "South African aesthetic", which showcased the work of a small number of artists who were trotted from "African" exhibition to "African" exhibition. In the process their work became so overdetermined with Western (and African) projections and fantasies of South Africa that the complex nature of artmaking in South Africa itself was virtually ignored in the international arena.

As either (or both) highly individual works or ambassadors of goodwill, the objects and installations that make up *Personal Affects* show the viewer that looking in New York was only part of the picture. The resulting works look everywhere – to the past, to the present, to religion, to politics, to oppression, to the body, to the media, to other art. The list goes on. And in this relentless looking, the work on view resides in places (or non-places) of uncertainty. It traffics in the uncanny, be it a swimmer who cannot swim or a white urban skateboarder who meets a black rural woman against a dreamscape of fabulous dancers.

It's impossible to overstate the importance that the Cathedral of St John the Divine played in the formation of artwork for this exhibition. Some of the main issues for the artists were dealing with the massive space, the rich ornament and the spectacle of the Cathedral itself. In the end, by dint of the artists' own thought processes, and by the location of such works in the Cathedral, many of the objects and installations had consciously religious overtones. Among the existing images of saints, virgins and martyrs were an unnamed saint, new virgins and fresh martyrs. Furthermore, for many of the artists, their works at the Cathedral were directly linked to those in the Museum. Cathedral installations such as Mustafa Maluka's *Tribute to Mr Devious* and Thando Mama's *1994 (II)* vacillated between art object and public memorial. As in the Cathedral's other memorials, viewers could place votive candles in front of these installations, and, at least in the case of Maluka's piece, were invited to do so. Seeing the art in the Cathedral, besides bringing a non-art-world audience to the South African work, focused viewers' attention on the art and decoration already installed in the Cathedral. This allowed viewers to look at the existing work with a new, enhanced or different perspective.

The Cathedral was a particularly fruitful place for artists to play with religious art, and for artists such as Wim Botha, Johannes Phokela, Claudette Schreuders, Clive van den Berg and Diane Victor, making work for the Cathedral enhanced the relationship between their practices and their respective explorations of the history of art, yielding objects in conversation with medieval, Renaissance, Baroque and/or other African forms. In these conversations, religious icons are bent around and their meanings thrown up for grabs in the artists' hands, showing not only the elastic nature of imagery, but also the constructed nature of religious metaphors. Moreover, the artists call up the porous boundary between icon and fetish.

Johannes Phokela, who has used Dutch Baroque technique and references in his practice for more than a decade, brings together the seventeenth century (the beginning of Dutch colonization in South Africa), contemporary painting and twenty-first century spectacle in his large-scale painting, *Apotheosis*. Quoting the performance artist and magician David Blaine, who was suspended in a glass box over London's Thames River for forty-four days in 2003, *Apotheosis,* in replacing Christ with the magician, explores the intersection of religion, colonialism, imperialism and commerce while it interrogates what Guy Debord called in 1967 "the society of the spectacle". Phokela also explores such intersections in his 1993 *Fall of the Damned* and *Diamonds and Bananas are Forever,* the latter playing directly upon the song performed by Marilyn Monroe in the 1953 film *Gentlemen Prefer Blondes*.

Wim Botha's *Mieliepap Pietà* reworks Michelangelo's 1498–1500 marble original in the maize meal that constitutes a staple food for some South Africans. The icon, in this sense, becomes more ambiguous. In the visual vocabulary of apartheid, particularly the widely circulated image of the dead body of Hector Petersen being carried away after the Soweto uprisings of 1976, the image, in both religious and political terms, speaks to a profound loss, martyrdom and mourning. In the Cathedral, the maize meal, instead of questioning the value of the icon, refashions it as a mark of loss felt in the artist's home as well as in the New York Cathedral.

Botha plays with icons and coats of arms in his work at the Museum, *Mnemonic Reconstruction*. Marked by a suspended fountain in which animals partake in an orgy, and bordered by drawings, a dripping etching and a panel of stained glass, the installation questions consciousness and plays with the viewer's perceptions of reality, while poking fun at the status normally conferred by coats-of-arms and other high-status symbols of identity.

Along similar lines, a sepulchre to an unnamed saint makes up Clive van den Berg's *Love's Ballast*. In the piece, there's a cyst on the saint's neck, which alludes to the exterior visualization of interior states. More specifically, the cyst, although a marker of disease, refers to love. The diseased body is then not a site to be disparaged, but rather, like the images of Mr Devious or the Pietà, a site for memorialization and the acknowledgement of trauma, loss and acceptance. *Love's Ballast* is directly tied to Van den Berg's sculpture at the Museum, *Family Tree II*. Out of the lower half of the body grows an armature embedded with thousands of small wooden pegs. These small tabs, or cysts if you will, are attached to acts of tabulation, counting and memorializing. Like *Love's Ballast, Family Tree* understands love and memorialization as active agents of change. *Family Tree,* moreover, alludes to families of choice, which gay people on both sides of the Atlantic often create after we come out of the closet.

Claudette Schreuders' trademark figural sculptures, in formal terms, share affinities with both the Colon figures of West Africa as well as police and political figures in the repertoire of South African "township art". However, Schreuders' objects in both the Cathedral and the Museum merge notions of icons and fetishes, and this merger serves as the foundation for the objects' evocative force. *The Free Girl,* in the Cathedral, conflates images of Mami Wata, a deity whose image is ubiquitous throughout West Africa, Central Africa and the Afro-Atlantic Diaspora, as well as the Virgin Mary. *The Free Girl* has a snake wrapped around her shoulder, as does Mami Wata, while she crushes another with her right foot, as does the Madonna. In this intersection, Schreuders explores stereotypical representations of women, and, like Botha and Phokela, attempts to question ingrained notions of whiteness (at least in an African context) and femininity. *Fetish,* in the Museum, is a smaller work that remakes a Kongo Nsiki figure into the body of a white woman. Like the African American artist Renée Stout's 1988 sculpture, *Fetish #2, Fetish* interrogates notions of the fetish, while, as in Van der Berg's work, the nail in the figure's arm, directly borrowed from the Nsiki, serves as an exterior visualization of inner turmoil.

Stereotypes of women, medieval decoration and iconic imagery serve as the foundation of Diane Victor's work in both venues. For the Museum, Victor made a triptych, entitled *Mater, Minder, Martyr*. In each of the images, Victor has taken a woman and placed her in a normally male-dominated role. In *Martyr,* the woman is recast as St Sebastian, and delineated on a paper imprinted (impregnated?) with images of sperm. Victor's deft substitution exposes the multiple readings available in any icon. Along the same lines, Victor's *Eight Mary's* in the Cathedral explore the roles of females in biblical narratives, at once questioning and critiquing the narrow range of representation of women in these images and texts. As in the Museum images, Victor attacks religious and gendered stereotypes by using these images as extensions of herself.

As Victor conflates herself with biblical narrative, so Churchill Madikida, also one of the exhibition curators, uses his own body as the site for critically thinking through Xhosa traditional practices, particularly circumcision, and cultural history, and his ambiguous relationship to these. His video *Struggles of the Heart* features Madikida himself, decked in the white powder associated with Xhosa ritual. In the piece, which shows only the artist's face, he is struggling to eat maize, which keeps coming out of his mouth. The maize, as signpost of tradition, alludes to Madikida's shifting identities among Xhosa people, South African, etc. The same dialectical movement is the subject of *Blood on My Hands,* which is at the Cathedral. Here, as in *Struggle,* Madikida thinks about shifting identities, but this particular piece is infused with histories of religion, colonialism and apartheid.

Such dialectical movement among differing subject positions is also the hallmark of Jay Pather's performances. Both *Hotel,* performed at the Museum, and his epic *From Before,* performed on the steps of the Cathedral at the opening, posit subjectivities as flexible and porous. As exegeses on what he sees as improbable cultural meetings, both performances think through culture not only as a sum of exterior signs and motives but also as constitutive of interior states of being. Moreover, in his performances, Pather's dancers explore the psychological manifestations of a desire that exists in taboo, and is mapped along interracial and intercultural lines.

The intercultural not only exists in the ways characters in a performance regard one another, but is also a staple of references made in most of the works on display. Most notably in this regard, Mustafa Maluka's memorial to his friend Mr Devious shows the cross-cultural importance of hip-hop culture as well as the makeshift memorial, which became a common feature of the New York City landscape in the aftermath of the attacks of September 11, 2001. Maluka's paintings are not straightforward portraits, they create iconic personalities, and in their formal and compositional qualities can be tied to both hip-hop and, like the work of British artist Chris Ofili, the popular Afro-culture of the 1970s.

The vast areas of pots used for cooking food during the annual Muslim festival of Eid, which celebrates the end of the fast of Ramadan, provide the foundation for Berni Searle's video *Vapour,* in which figures zigzag around pots that ostensibly contain cooking food. As in Searle's earlier works, food and its preparation are connected to the construction of subjectivity and issues of belonging. However, here, what the viewer finds is not an attempt to define identity through food, but rather disillusionment at the bottom of Searle's pots. In its position at the entrance to the Cathedral's Baptistry and Columbarium, *Vapour* becomes overlaid with the beginnings and endings of life. *Vapour* leaves us with nothing but ashes, which, in the Columbarium, represent the remains of those who have entered it.

Samson Mudzunga's drums are larger parts of performances, entitled *Suka Africa Fundudzi,* that explore artistic freedom and, like the work of Maluka, Searle and, to a certain degree, Pather, are steeped in understanding the transformative qualities of ritual. In each of the two drums Mudzunga carved, he enacted a performance in which he is put into the drum under lock and key. While musicians play and people dance, Mudzunga emerges from the drum free of his chains and dressed in different clothes. With its metaphors of baptism and rebirth, Mudzunga's performance points to his artistic transformation as well as his artistic (and literal) freedom.

Related to Searle's ashes are Sandile Zulu's four elements. In both venues, Zulu's work incorporates earth, air, fire and water to interrogate histories of belonging and dispossession. Burn marks on canvases, the erratic grids Zulu makes in his practice, tears in his canvases, the smell of smoke and ash, and installations of stones and red ribbons posit the four elements not only as the foundation of all matter, but also, as for the Greek philosophers, as the source of emotions. On Zulu's twisting and turning canvases, the four elements are also attached to sentient activity, and on that level they can be seen as the place from which all action emanates. As such, Zulu's invocation of the elements is a way to articulate a history of political struggle and protest and, in their relationship to the land, to express both belonging and dispossession.

The residue of apartheid takes centre stage in Thando Mama's installations. *1994 (I)*, which consists of double projected video pieces, places the artist's body in a conversation with the history of apartheid and its aftermath. Part of the same piece, *1994 (II)*, which occupies its own chapel within the Cathedral, features forty-six drawings on glass, each item representing a year of legislated apartheid and its dismantling between 1990 and 1994. Mama's work makes this political history tangible, and in a sense his pieces function as a kind of private archive of one person's subjective, yet largely second-hand, recollection of the period.

The vestiges of apartheid, and continued oppression even after the introduction of democracy, are important in Steven Cohen's *Chandelier* piece. In an unlikely meeting between a gender-bending performance artist as human chandelier and homeless black people in an about-to-be-razed informal settlement in Johannesburg, Cohen, in seven-inch-high fetish heels with Stars of David attached to his forehead, wanders around the settlement, engaging residents and becoming a living spectacle. Cohen's work, in its bringing together of performance art, camp (in the transgressive sense of Susan Sontag), the informal settlement, Hollywood glamour, and the club kid aesthetic embodied by gender-bending impresarios Michael Alig, James St James in the 1980s and 90s, sought to show that discrimination and oppression, while not the same everywhere, nevertheless cut across racial, sexual and religious lines. In each venue (a video of the performance played in both), different things came through in different ways. In the Cathedral, religion came through much more powerfully than it did in the Museum, where it played in the artist's *Boudoir*, in the midst of his own things, making the piece far more autobiographical.

Like Cohen, Minnette Vári's work also resides in defamiliarization and a sense of the uncanny. *Cyclops* forces the viewer to look through the mouth of a face coming out of the gallery wall. What the viewer sees is a mandala, which is in fact a dystopic kaleidoscopic space that features chaos, further emphasized by the audio portion of the piece, and the very deformation of the body through its constant reconfiguration. Her 2003 video projection, *The Calling*, explores the psychological links between Johannesburg and New York that exist for her. Constructed from footage from both cities as well as Brussels, the video rests in the desire to be in utopia. Moreover, the viewer is implicated in the projections by the presence of shadows from the Cathedral itself. Yet at the same time, the viewer, like the artist, who is herself featured as a gargoyle that knows everything but tells nothing, finds herself in the world of the uncanny, a kind of no-place.

Robin Rhode's *Autonomous Drawing Project,* a small-scale presentation of slides of found objects from around New York and drawings made in response to them, explores the artist's childhood memories of attachments to materials as well as his observations of New Yorkers' connections to the furniture they throw away. Alongside the objects, Rhode makes drawings that show one how to reuse the items. Rhode's use of drawings and photographs of the objects under scrutiny allow for an investigation of cultural differences that finds its genesis in lived experience and commodity culture.

As do gargoyles, Jane Alexander's trademark humanoid figures reside in the arena of the grotesque. Like her works over the past two decades, the characters that populate her work in this exhibition directly allude to issues of surveillance, the threat of violence, blood and more abstract decentering of perception. In the Cathedral, Alexander has made a religious tableau that refers to Psalm 51, the prayer for the remission of sins. In her continued invocation of the grotesque in her work, Alexander continues to allude to the interior disfiguring caused by external actions.

Doreen Southwood's bodies, while not grotesque, refer to incongruity and point out the unreliability of reality. Southwood's *Swimmer*, while perched on a diving board, cannot swim. The drain in her side makes such an action impossible. Such states of dis-ease are further amplified by *Ribbon Pillars,* in the Museum, and her 2003 *Black Hole,* in the Cathedral. Each of these pieces creates a space that is difficult to navigate. *Ribbon Pillars* suggests that four ribbon columns are functioning as true architectural elements, when, in fact, they are not. The ceiling they seem to hold up could fall at any moment. *Black Hole* is indecipherable. As one tourist said in the Cathedral, "looks like there's water on it." These unstable bodies and unstable spaces, like the work of Botha, play the "real" in ways that attempt to decentre our physical and emotional selves.

As I stated earlier, *Personal Affects* begs to be understood as post- a number of things. In her essay in part one of the catalogue, Liese van der Watt attempts to get her readers to understand the works in the Museum for African Art and the Cathedral of St John the Divine within current theoretical debates that problematize 1980s and 1990s identity politics. [2] In fact, she works very hard to loosen up issues of identity and of race (although gender, class, sexual orientation and national affiliation are never brought explicitly into the conversation). Van der Watt's points are well taken, but by her own admission, post- serves to underscore the importance of the thing described.[3] In other words, post-identity reaffirms identity. Post-black, which foreclosed any possibility of discussing the actual artwork that was made for the *Freestyle* exhibition, recentres not some abstract notion of race, but blackness. Moreover, post-black perhaps designates more accurately a particular generation of post-civil rights artists than it does a new theoretical viewpoint. What I'm getting at is this: many of the works in *Personal Affects* are emotional exegeses that *are* about race, that *are* about identity. But they are also about more than any one of those things. It seems to me, moreover, that in this arena the term that really needs to be deconstructed is "South Africa", and what needs to be addressed is the conundrum of individual artists claiming national and transnational affiliations simultaneously. Perhaps this means a post-South Africa? I don't know. But what it could mean is a breakdown of "South Africa" as a mode of reception in the international art world.

Steven Nelson, Assistant Professor of African and African American art history at the University of California, Los Angeles, is the Magalen O Bryant International Fellow at the Radcliffe Institute for Advanced Study at Harvard University for 2004-5. Professor Nelson received his PhD in the History of Art and Architecture from Harvard University in 1998. He has published on African art, architecture and urbanism, African American art history, and Queer Studies. He is former Reviews Editor for *Art Journal* and former Contributing Editor to *African Arts*. His book, titled *From Cameroon to Paris: Mousgoum Architecture and the Making of Meaning,* is currently under review at the University of Chicago Press. He is working on a second book manuscript, entitled *Dakar: The Making of an African Metropolis.* Nelson also holds a BA in Studio Art from Yale University.

1. See Rasheed Araeen, "What is Post-Apartheid South Africa and its Place in the World" in *Africus: Johannesburg Biennale* (Johannesburg: Transitional Metropolitan Council, 1995), pp 16–19.
2. See Liese van der Watt, "Towards an 'Adversarial Aesthetics': A Personal Response to Personal Affects" in Sophie Perryer (ed), *Personal Affects: Power and Poetics in Contemporary South African Art* (New York and Cape Town: Museum for African Art and Spier, 2004), pp 45-54.
3. Van der Watt, p 47.

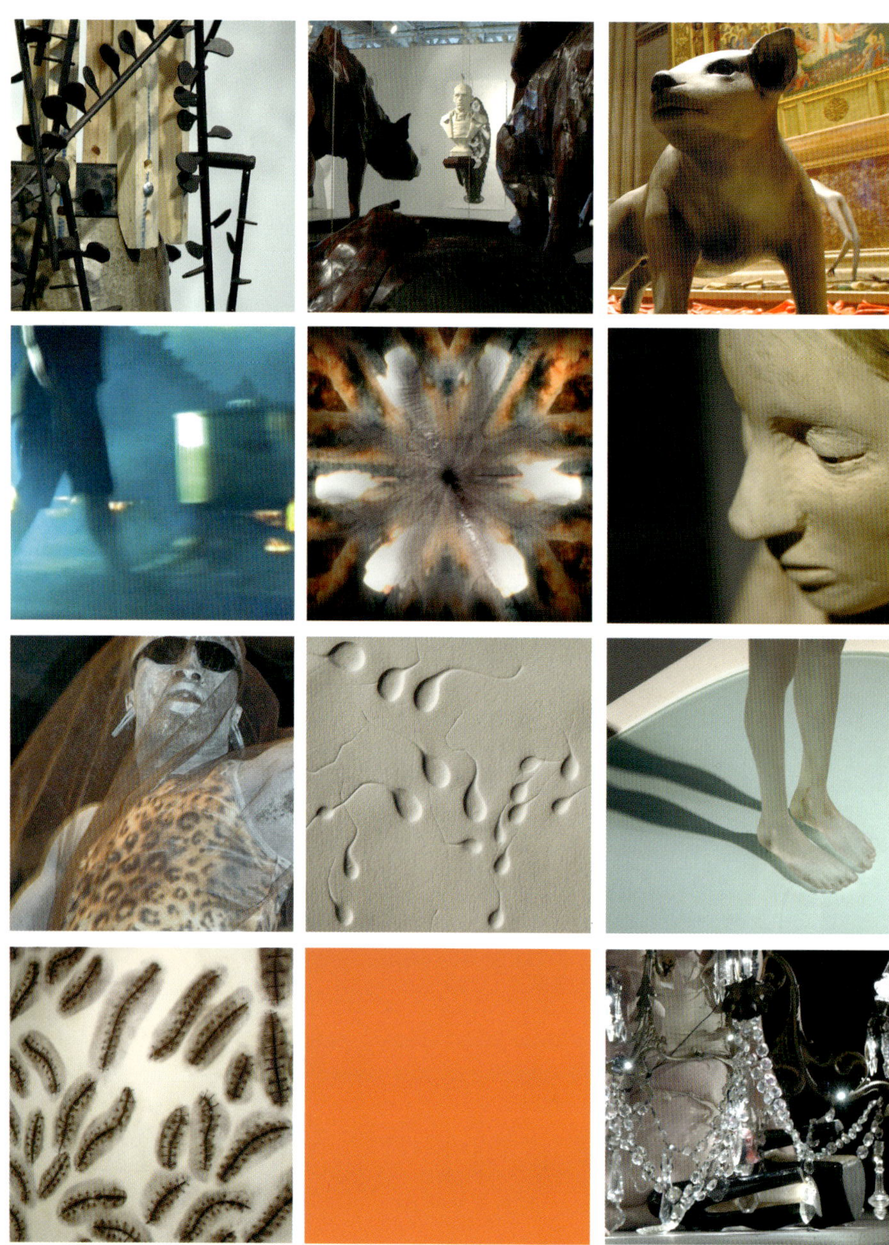

THE ARTISTS

Installation views at the Cathedral of St John the Divine
and the Museum for African Art, New York

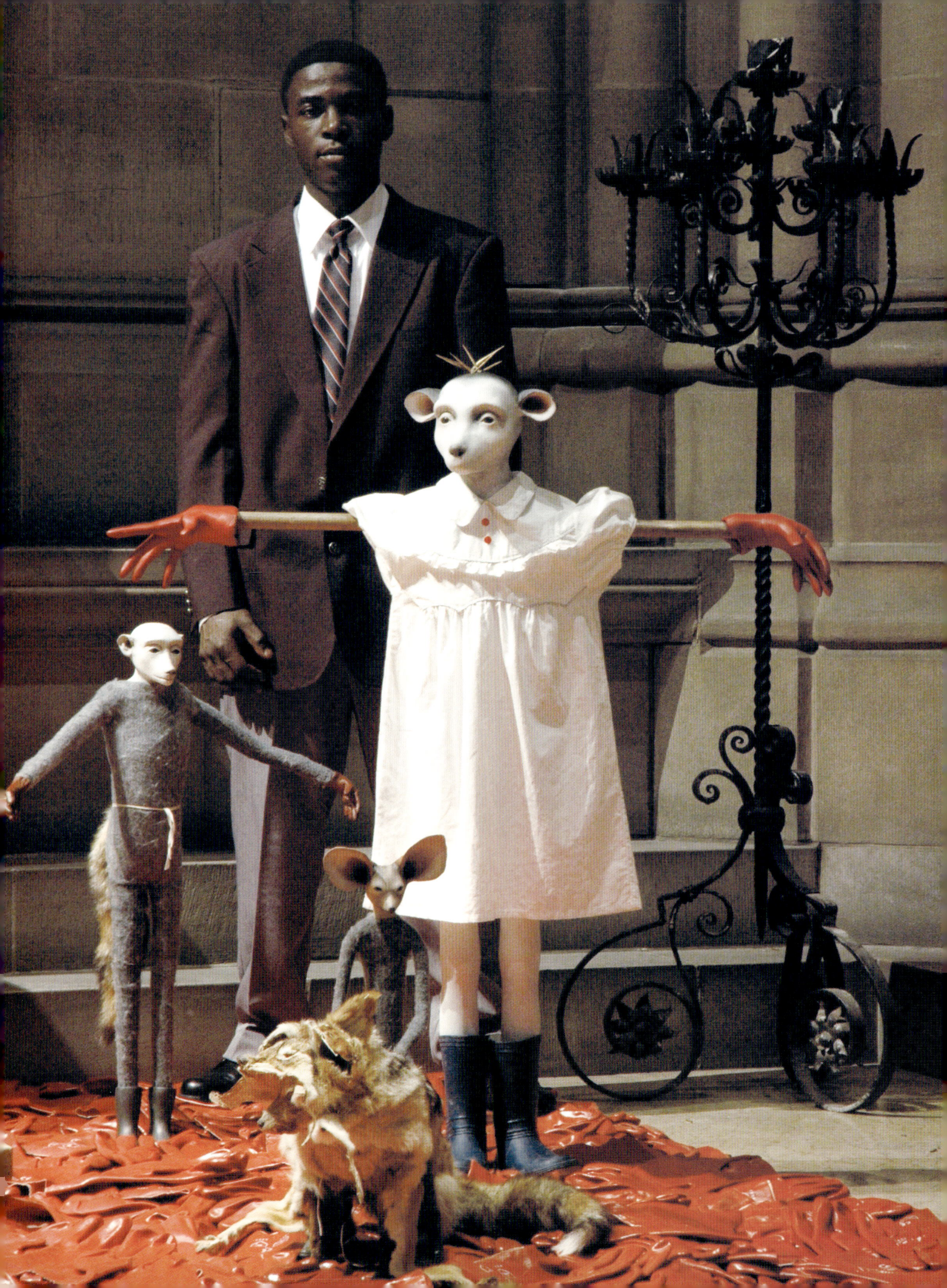

JANE ALEXANDER

these pages and overleaf
The sacrifices of God are a troubled spirit
2002–2004
Mixed media installation including Hobbled ruminant with rider,
Harbinger with protective boots, Bird, Small beast, Guardian,
Bat-eared doll riding a bat-eared fox wearing a black-backed jackal skin,
and Lamb with stolen boots
All Souls Bay, Cathedral of St John the Divine, 2004

Courtesy of the artist
Artist's acknowledgements: Riedoh Allen, John Nankin, Abraham Theron

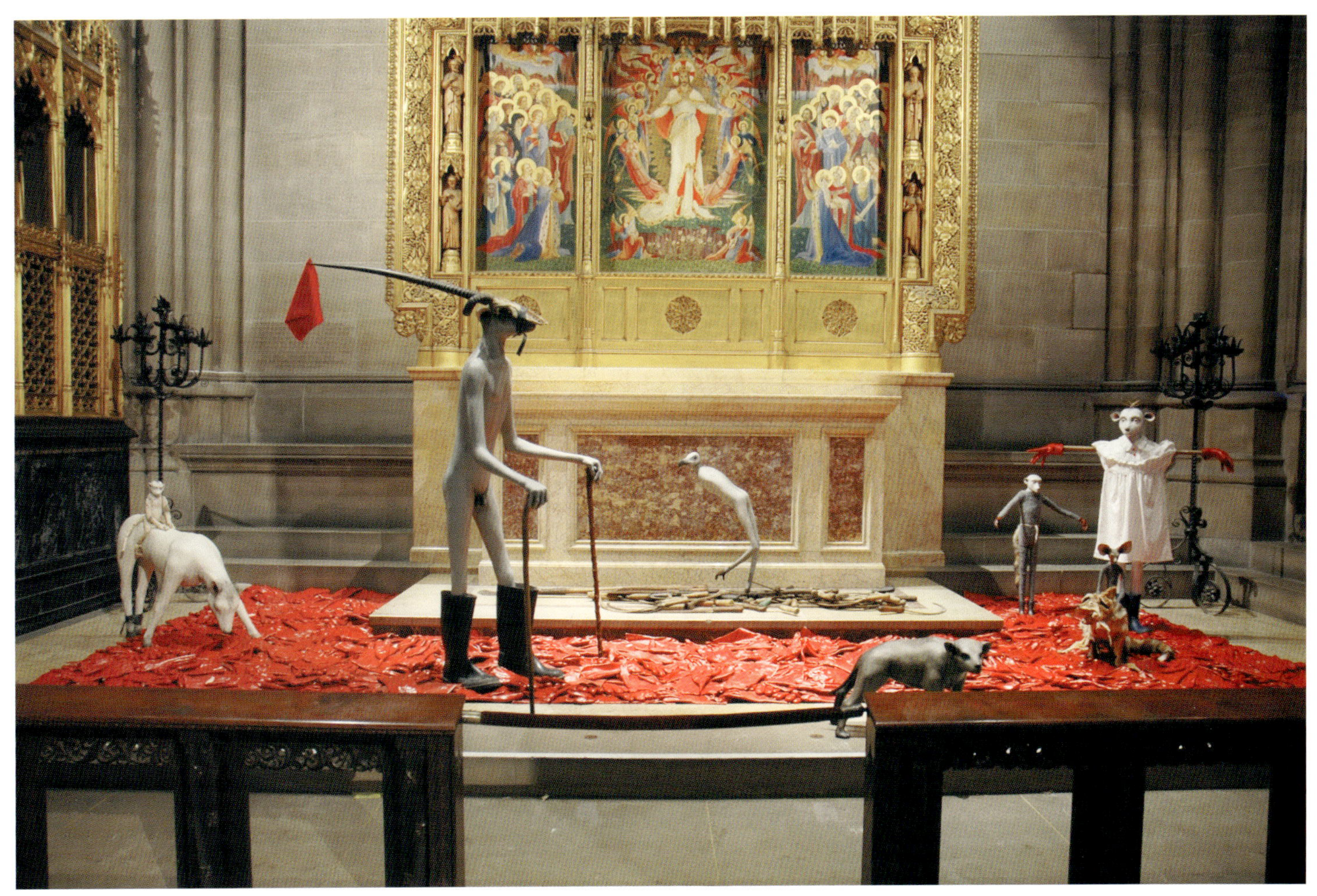

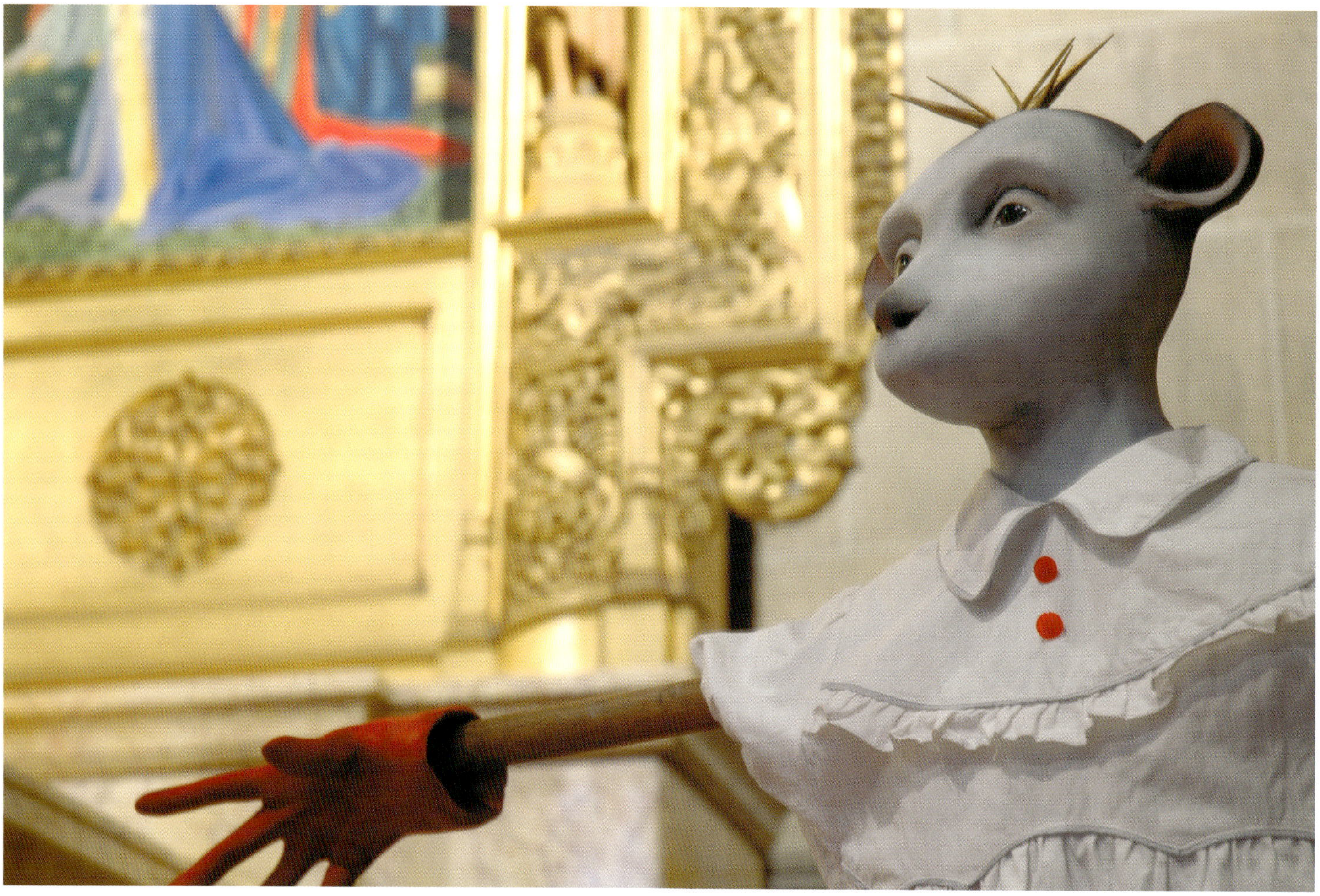

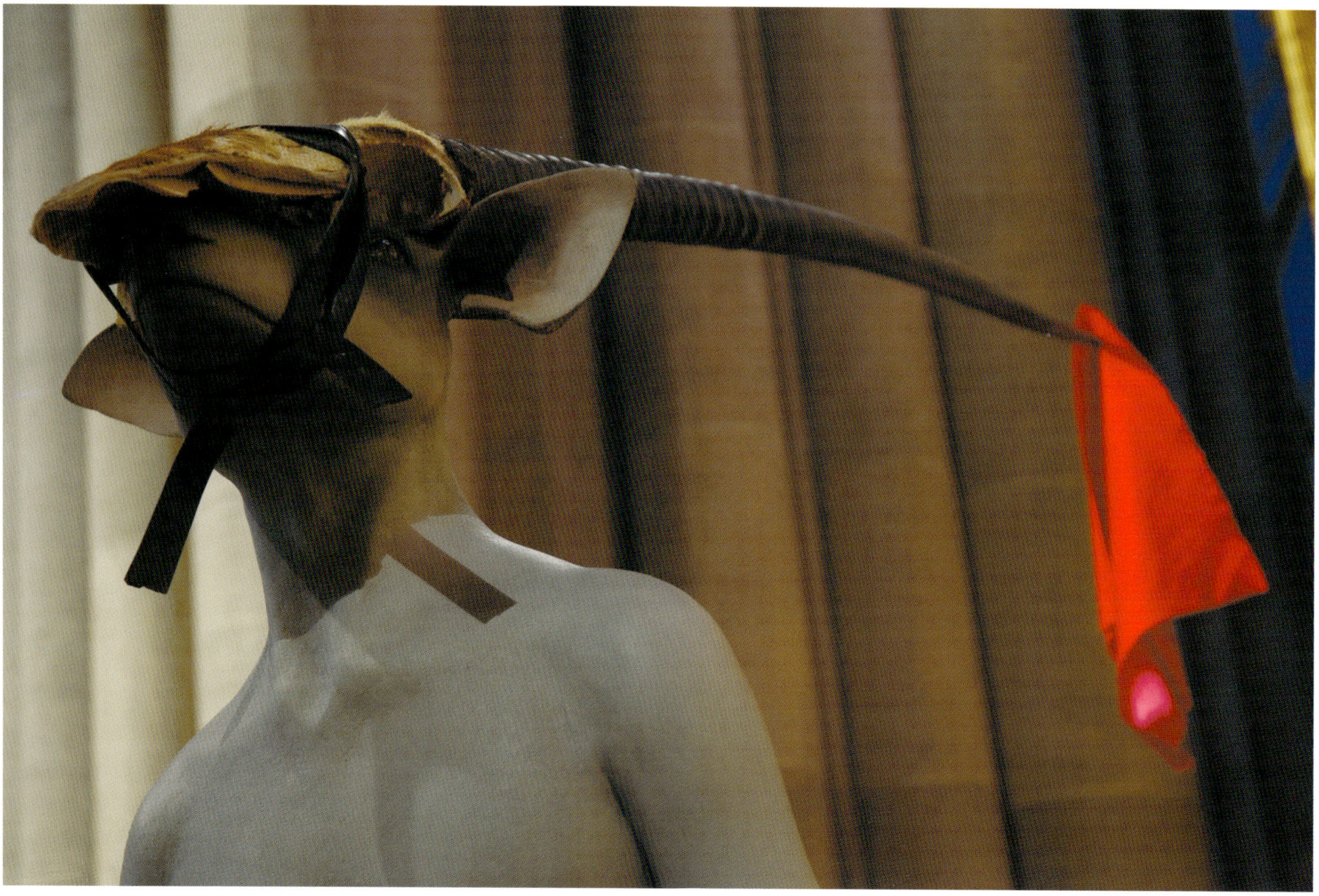

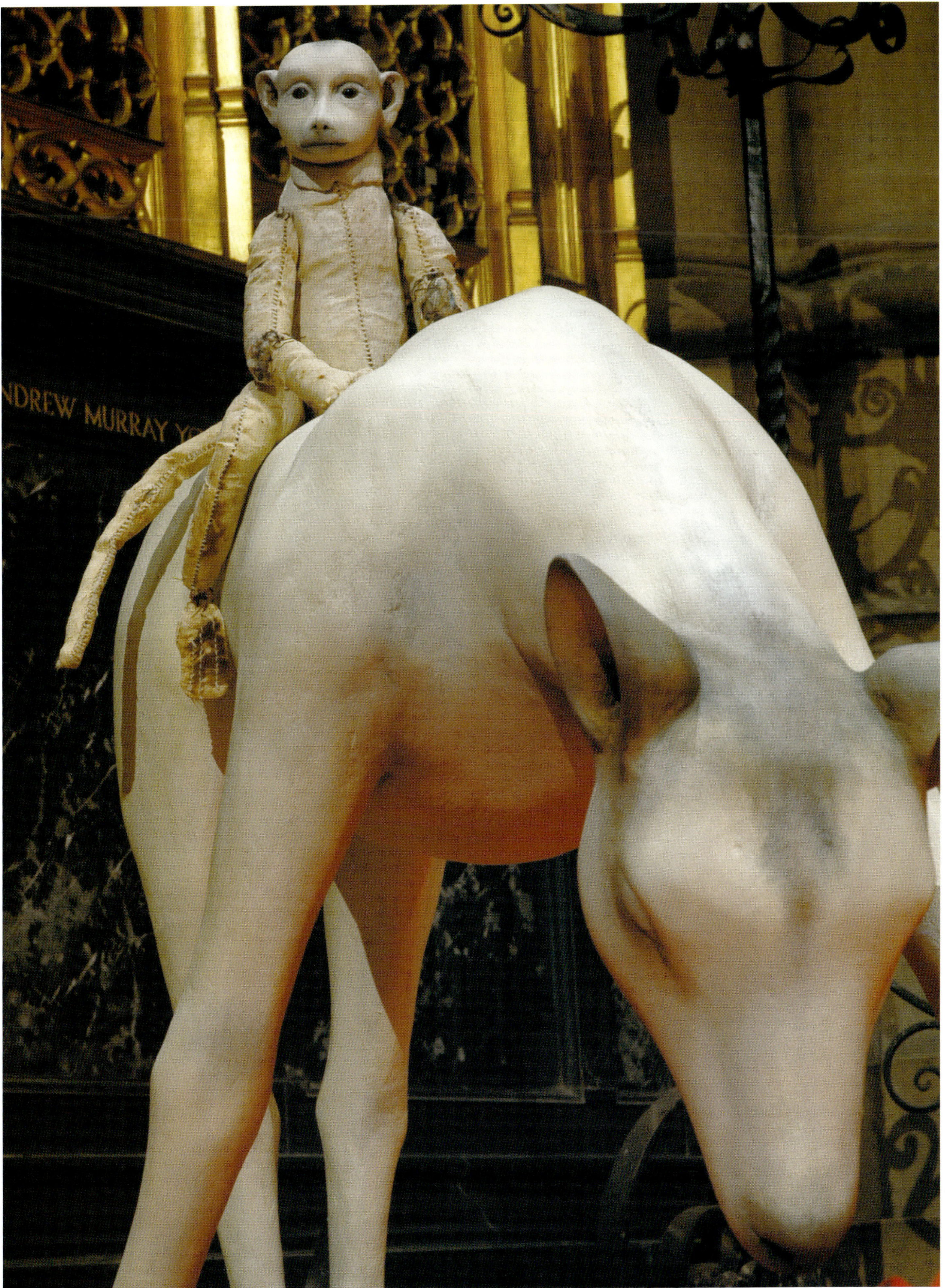
NDREW MURRAY Y

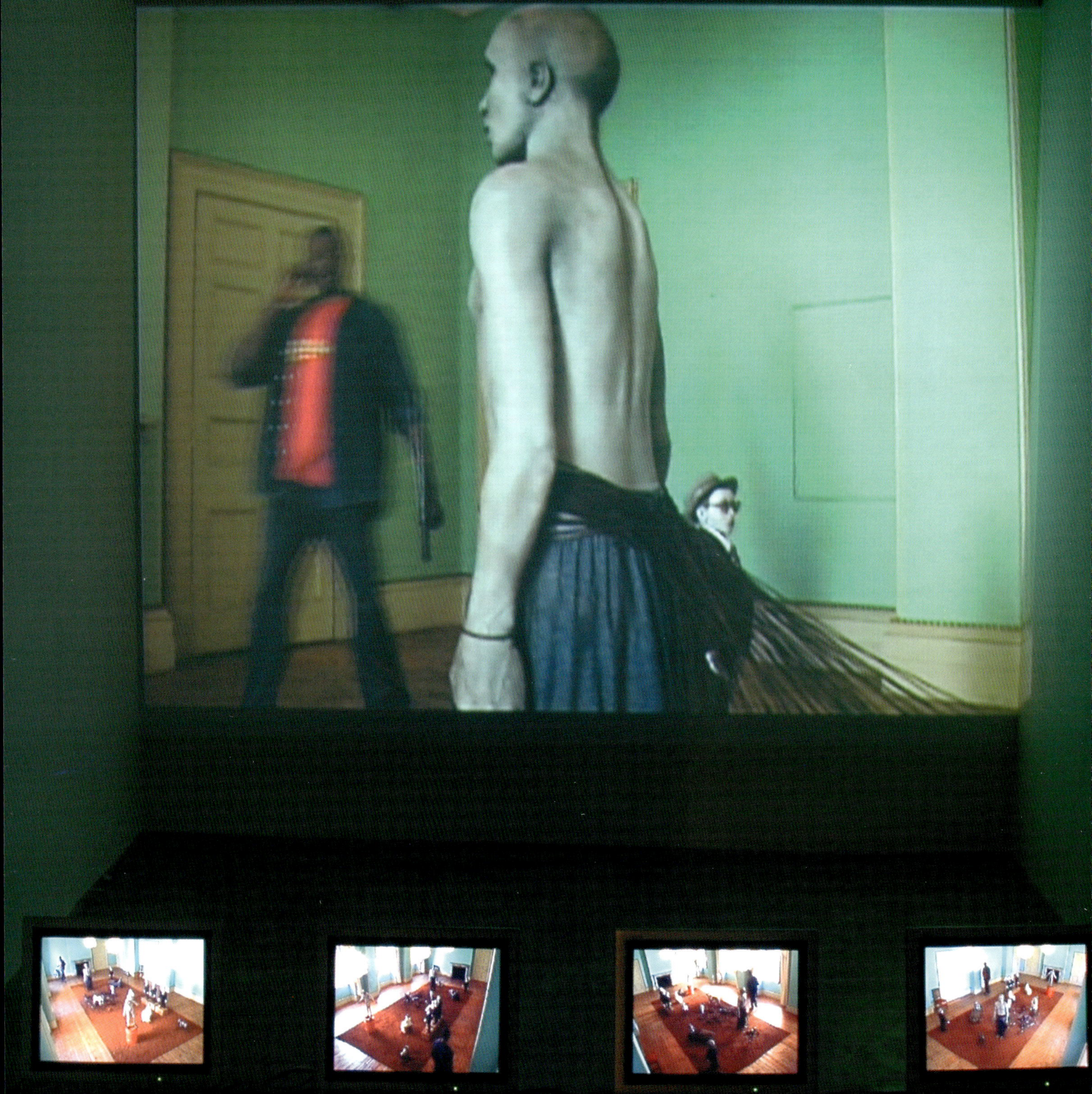

African Adventure
The British Officers' Mess
Castle of Good Hope, Cape Town
30 January 2002
2002–2004
Video projection (camera: Craig Matthew) and LCD monitors with security camera footage
Museum for African Art, 2004

Courtesy of the artist
Artist's acknowledgements: Nick Kalle, Khangelani Mzamo, John Nankin, Abraham Theron, Edward Young

this page, left
Vissershok
2001
Digital photomontage, pigment print on cotton paper
29.5 X 40 CM

Courtesy of the artist

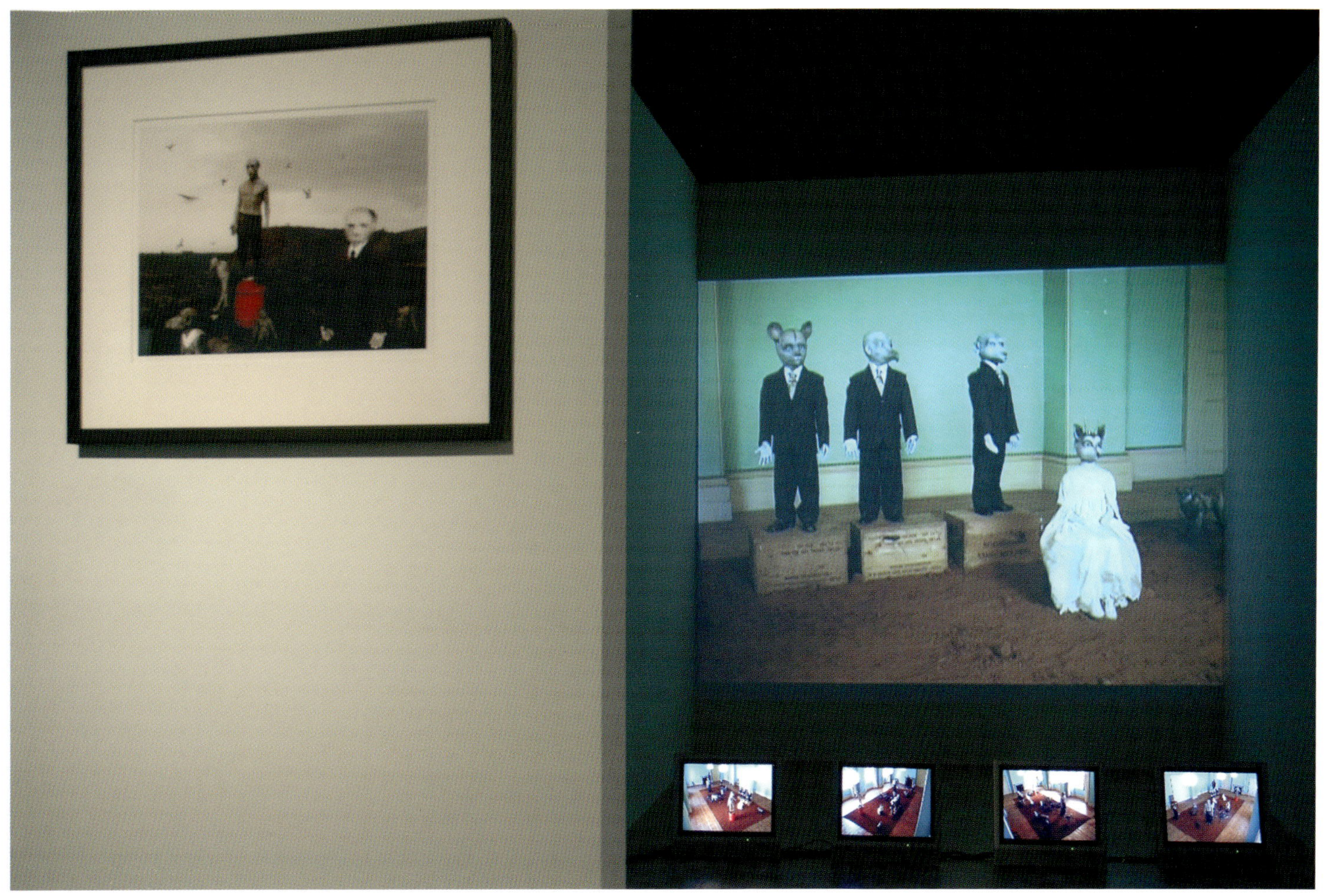

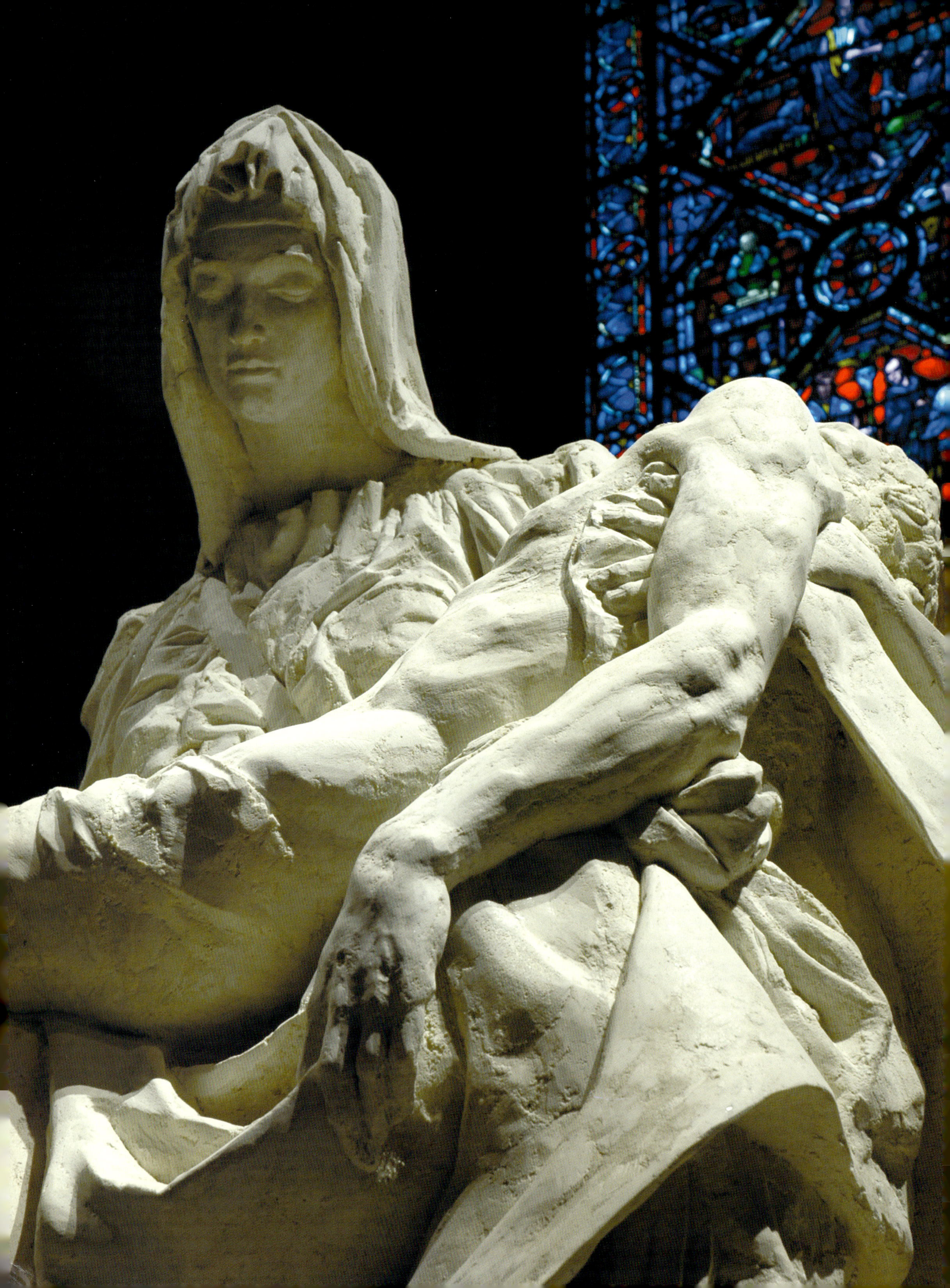

WIM BOTHA

Mieliepap Pietà (Maize Meal Pietà)
2004
Maize meal and resin
DIMENSIONS IDENTICAL TO MICHELANGELO'S PIETÀ:
HEIGHT 174 CM, WIDTH AT BASE 195 CM
Press Bay, Cathedral of St John the Divine, 2004

Courtesy of Spier, Cape Town

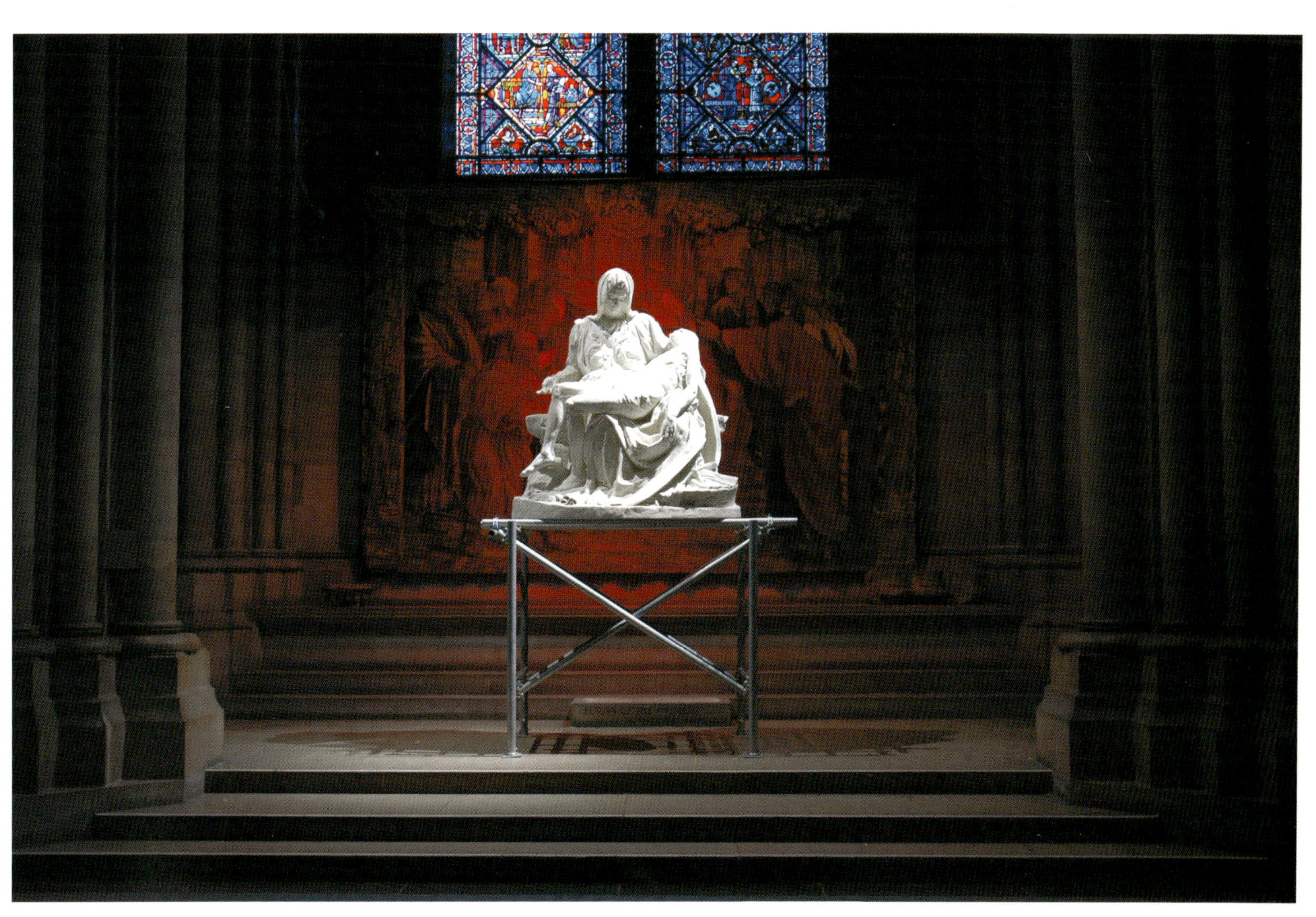

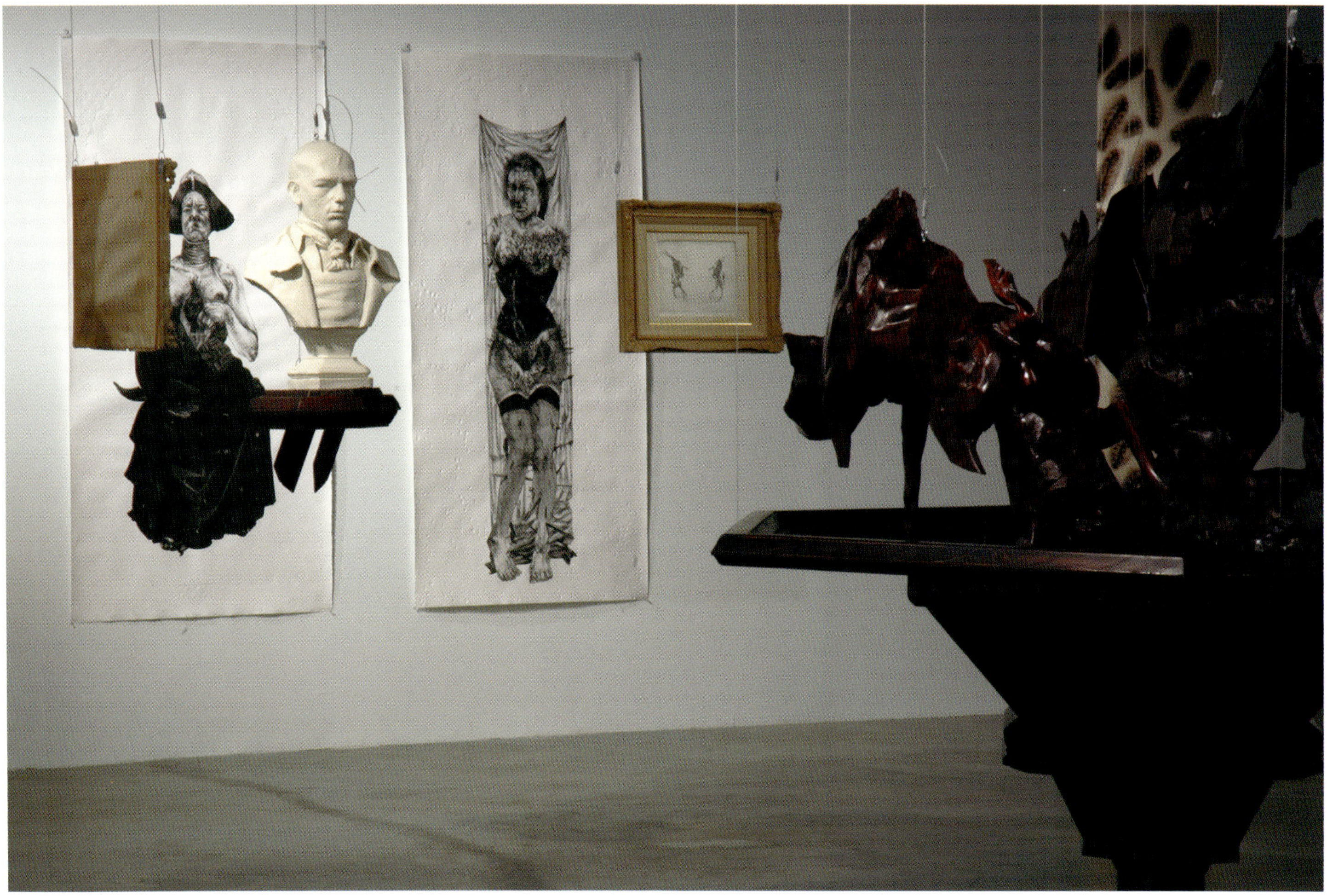

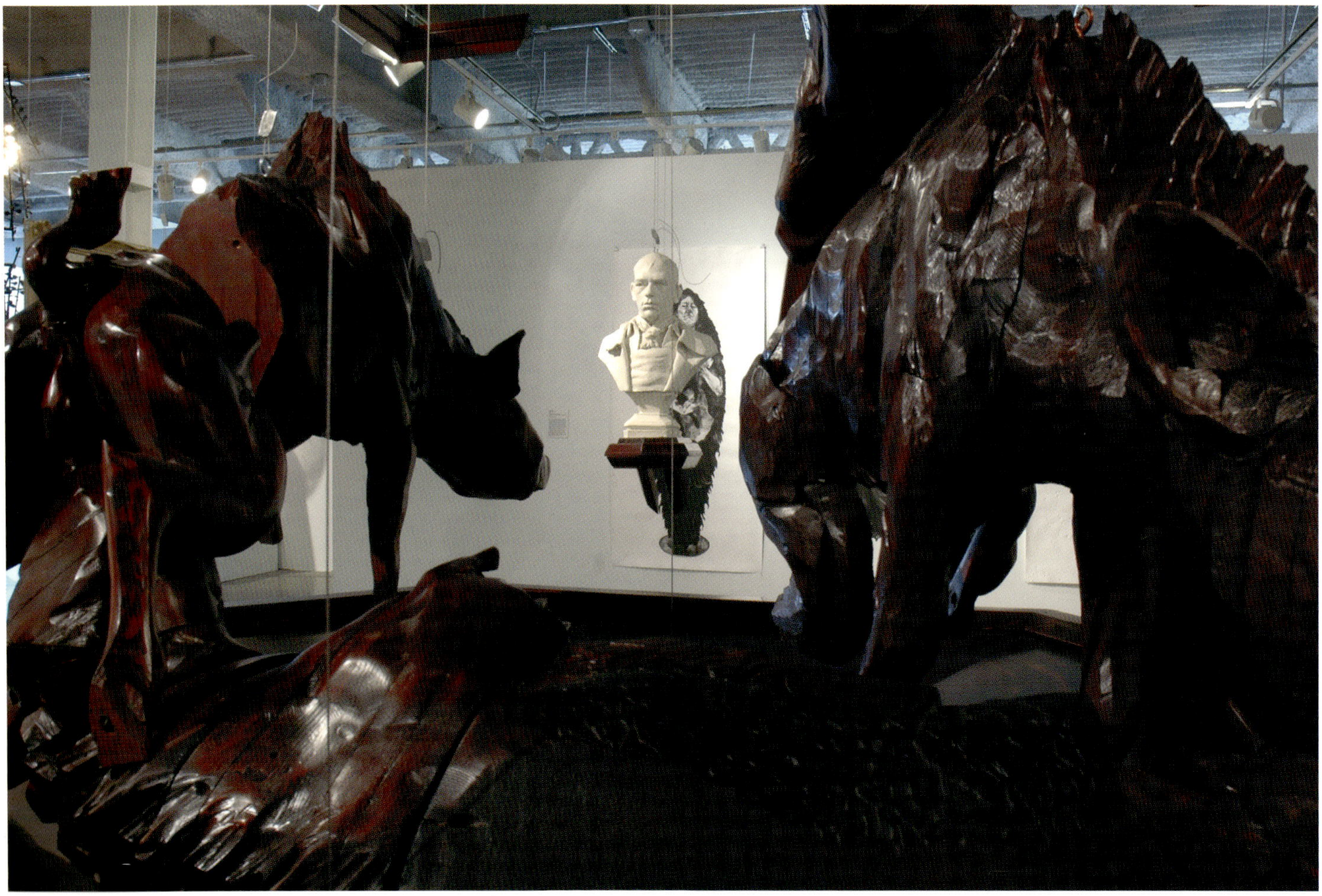

Mnemonic Reconstruction
2004
Simulated found objects: wood, glass, lead, cast resin frames, etchings
LIFESIZE, INSTALLATION DIMENSIONS VARIABLE
Museum for African Art, 2004

Commissioned by *Season South Africa* for *Personal Affects*
Courtesy of the artist and Michael Stevenson Contemporary

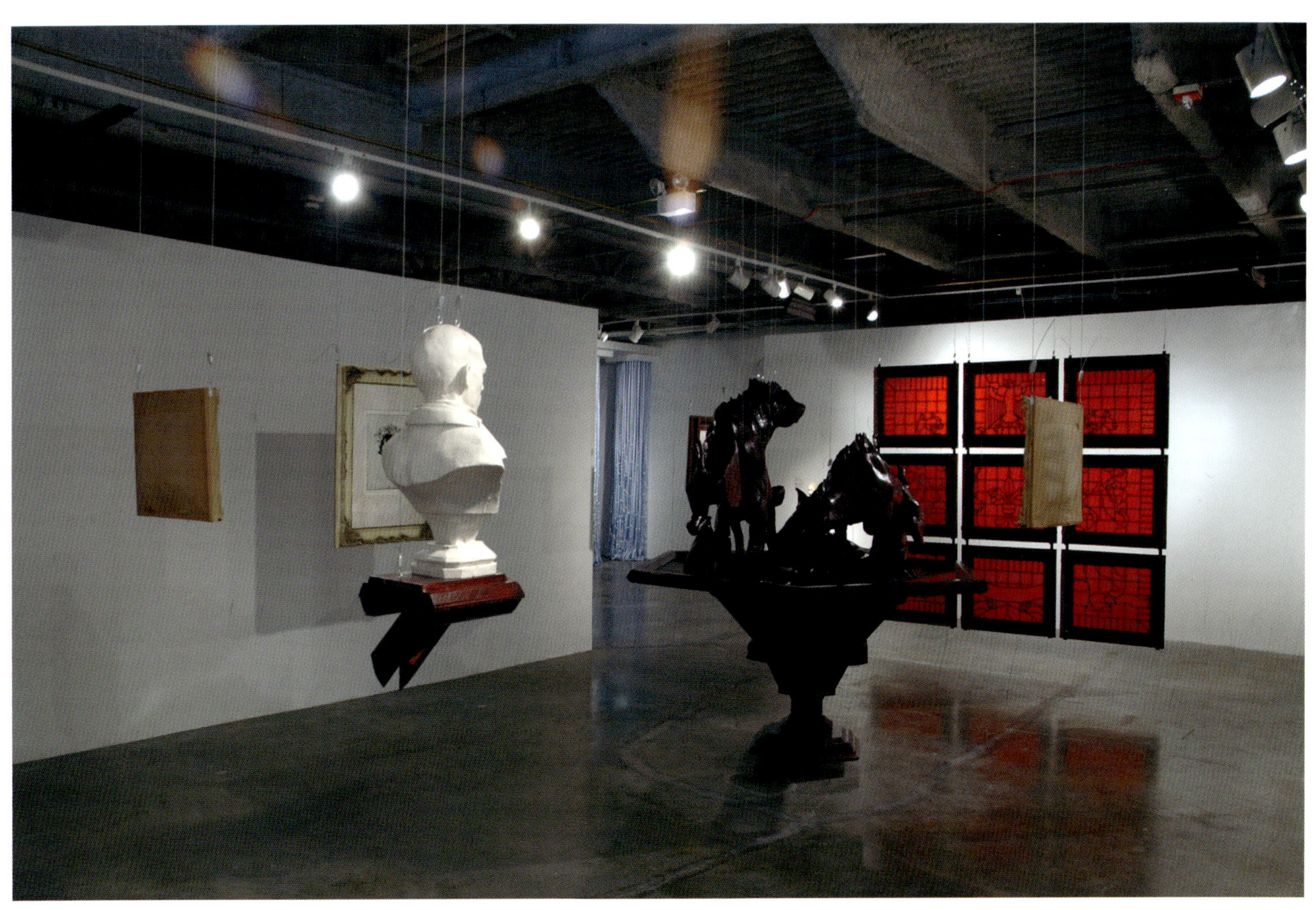

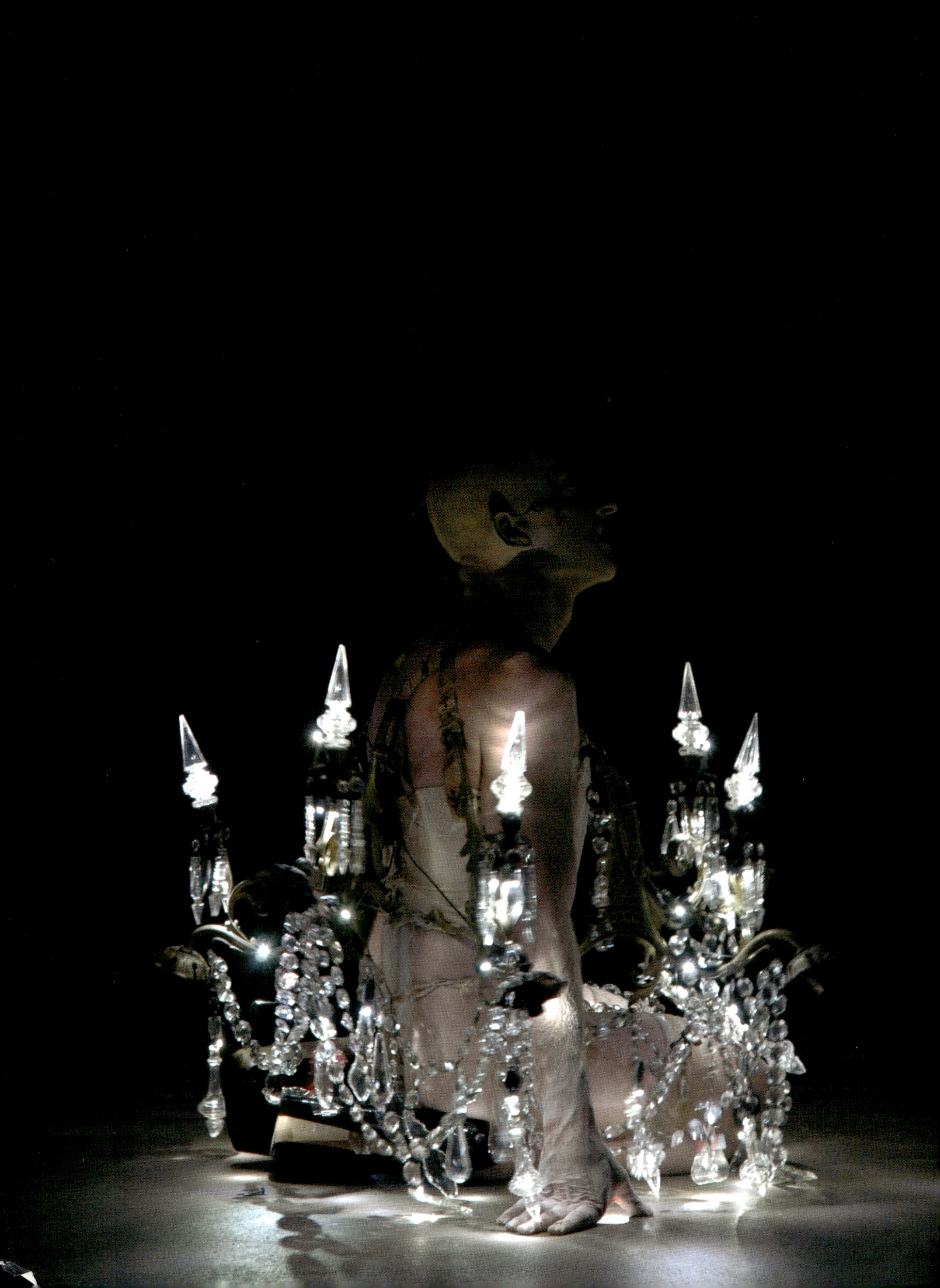

STEVEN COHEN

Chandelier
2002–2004
Performance
The Crossing, Cathedral of St John the Divine, 23 September 2004

The artist's participation in *Personal Affects* is courtesy
of the Ballet Atlantique/Régine Chopinot, France

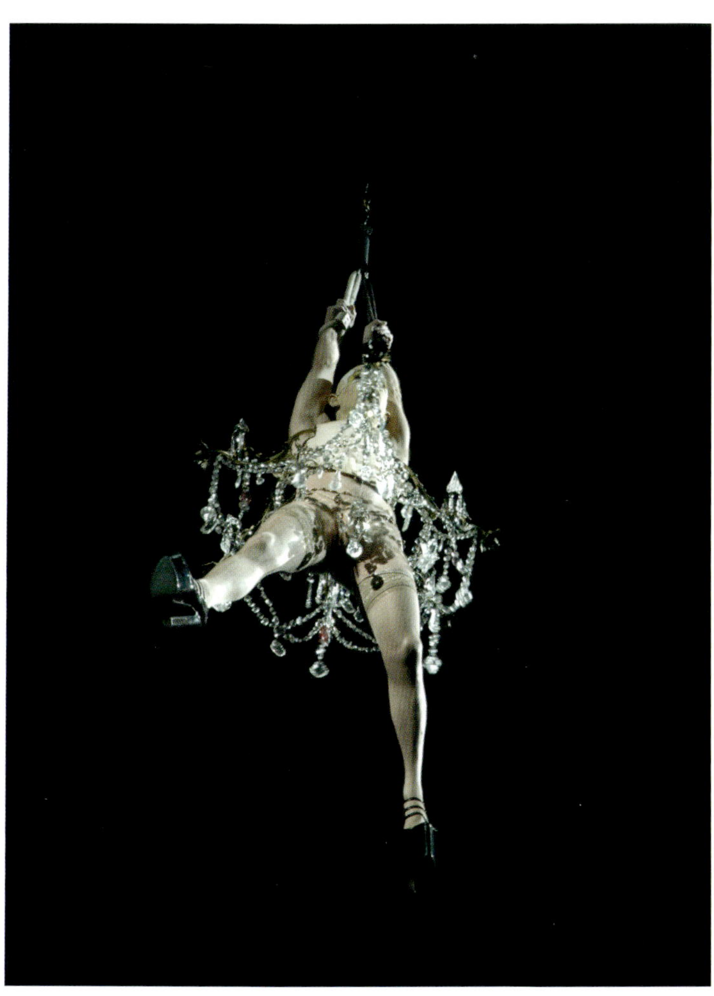
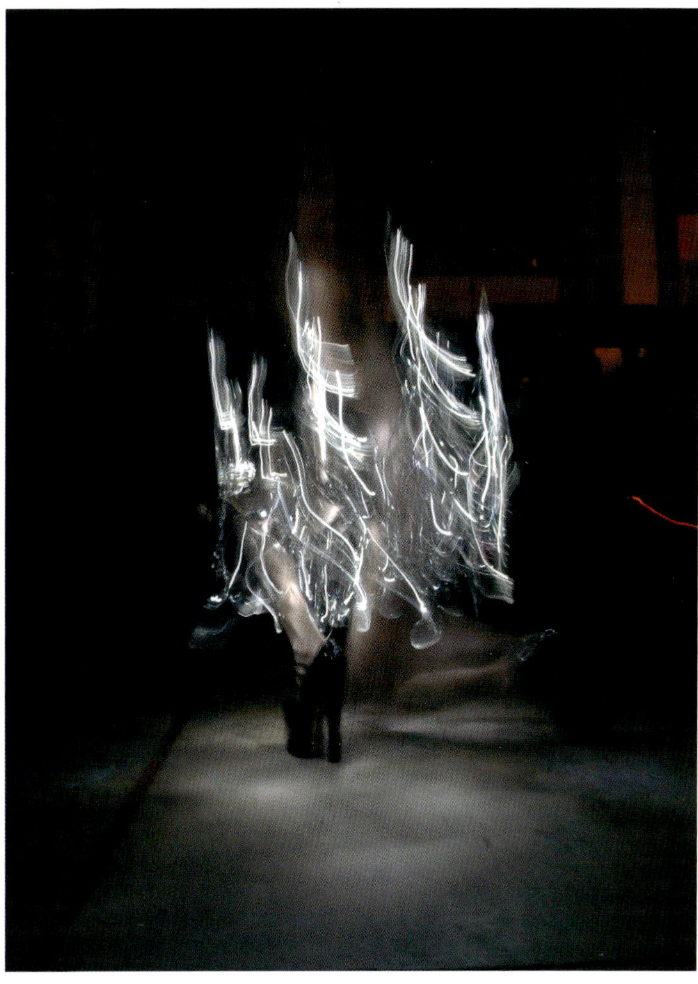

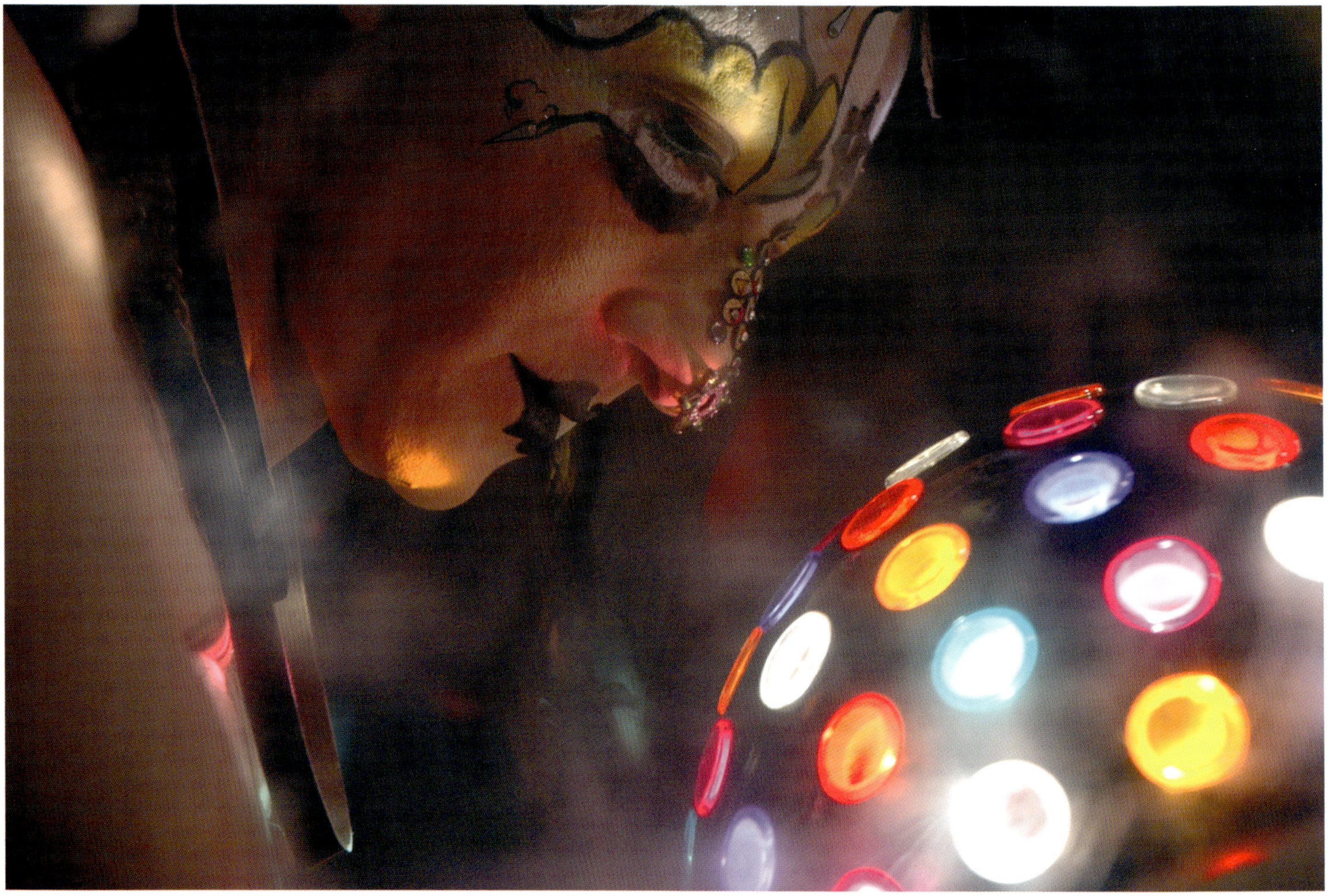

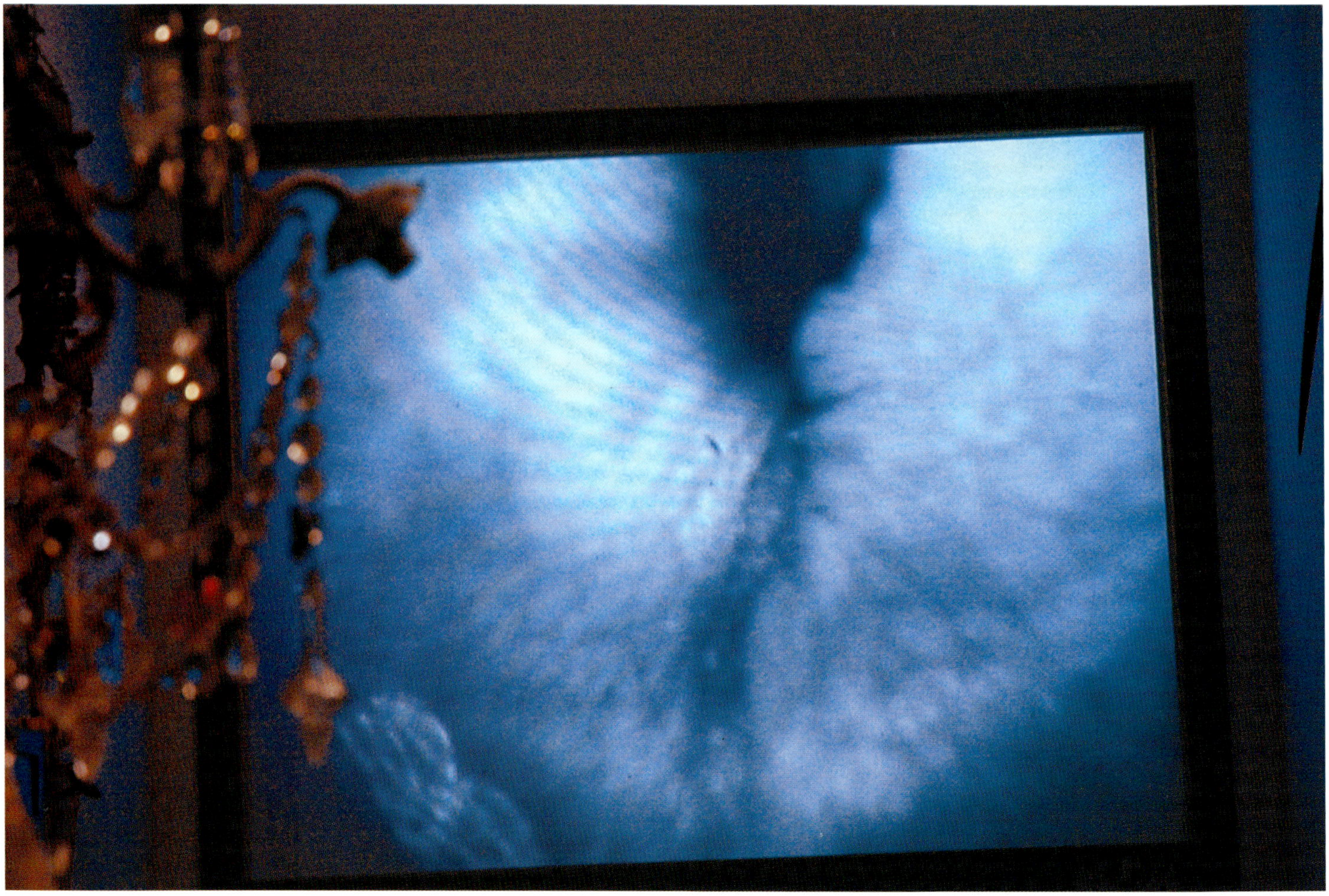

Free Jew is cheap at twice the price
2004
Performance using the human body, found objects,
micro-camera and video projection
Museum for African Art, 21 September 2004

The artist's participation in *Personal Affects* is courtesy
of the Ballet Atlantique/Régine Chopinot, France

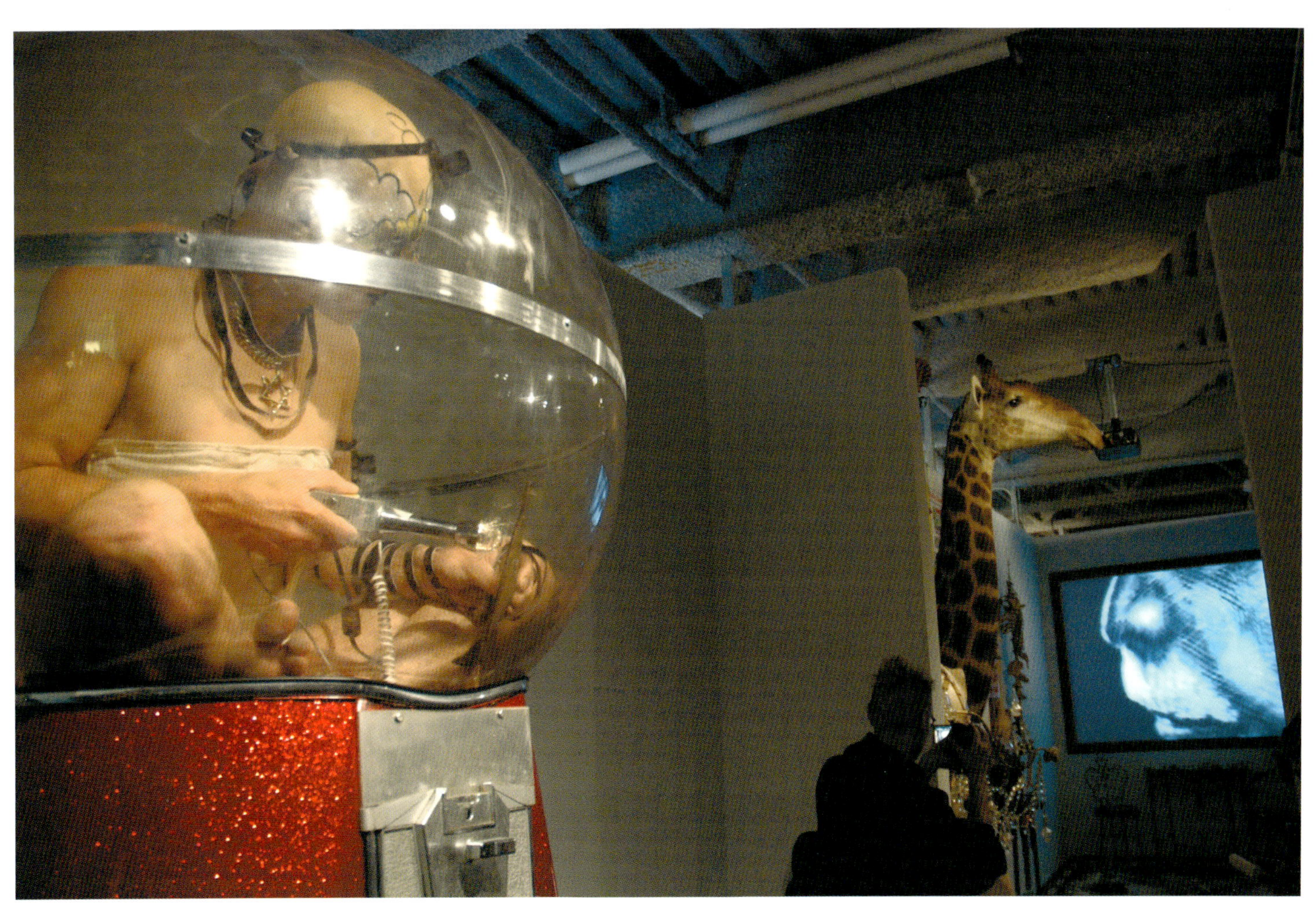

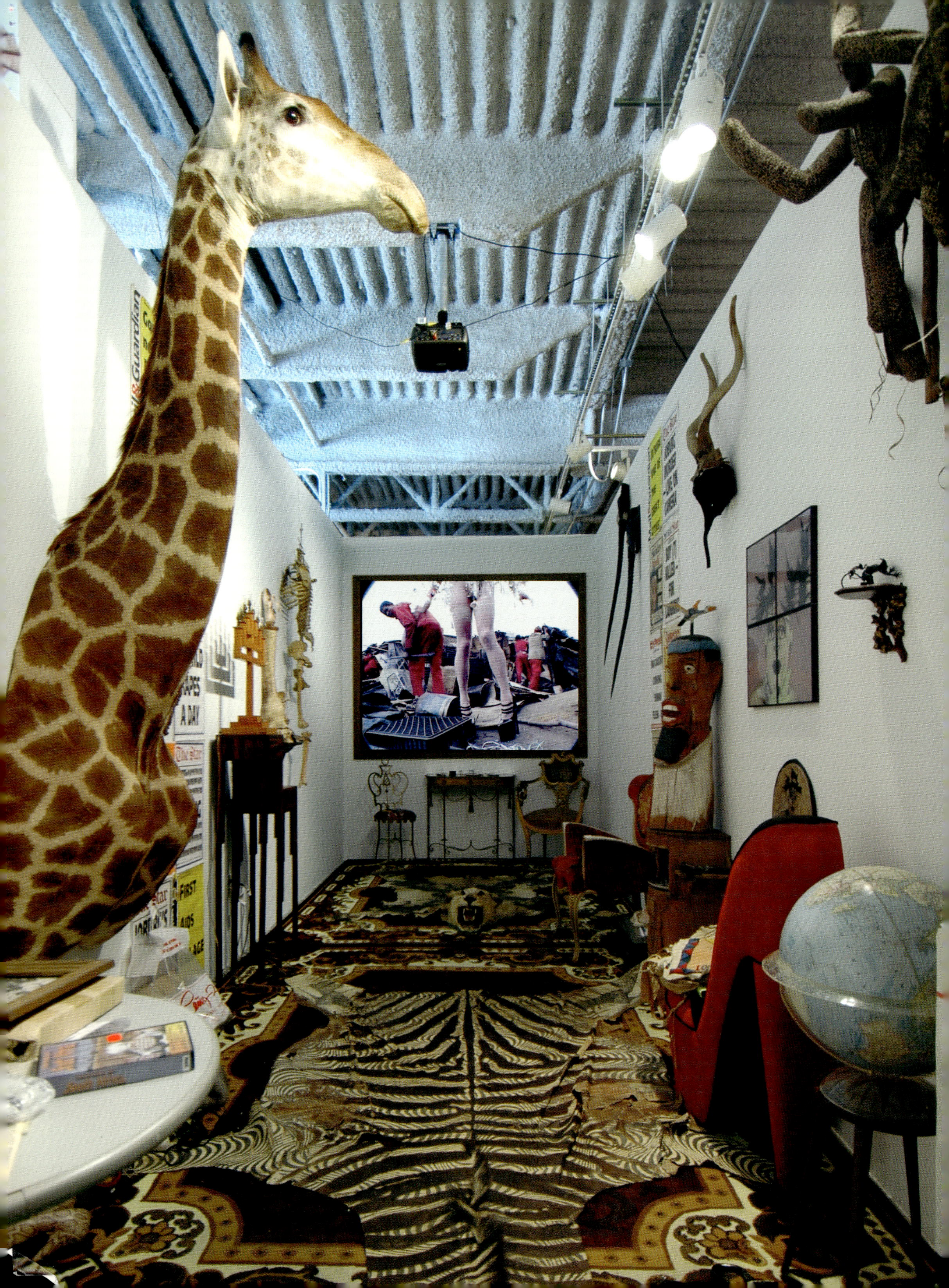

Boudoir
2004
Installation with objects from the collection of the artist and Chandelier, *2002,*
video of public intervention in shack settlement, Newtown, Johannesburg
VIDEO DURATION 16 MIN 37 SEC
Museum for African Art, 2004

Commissioned by *Season South Africa* for *Personal Affects*

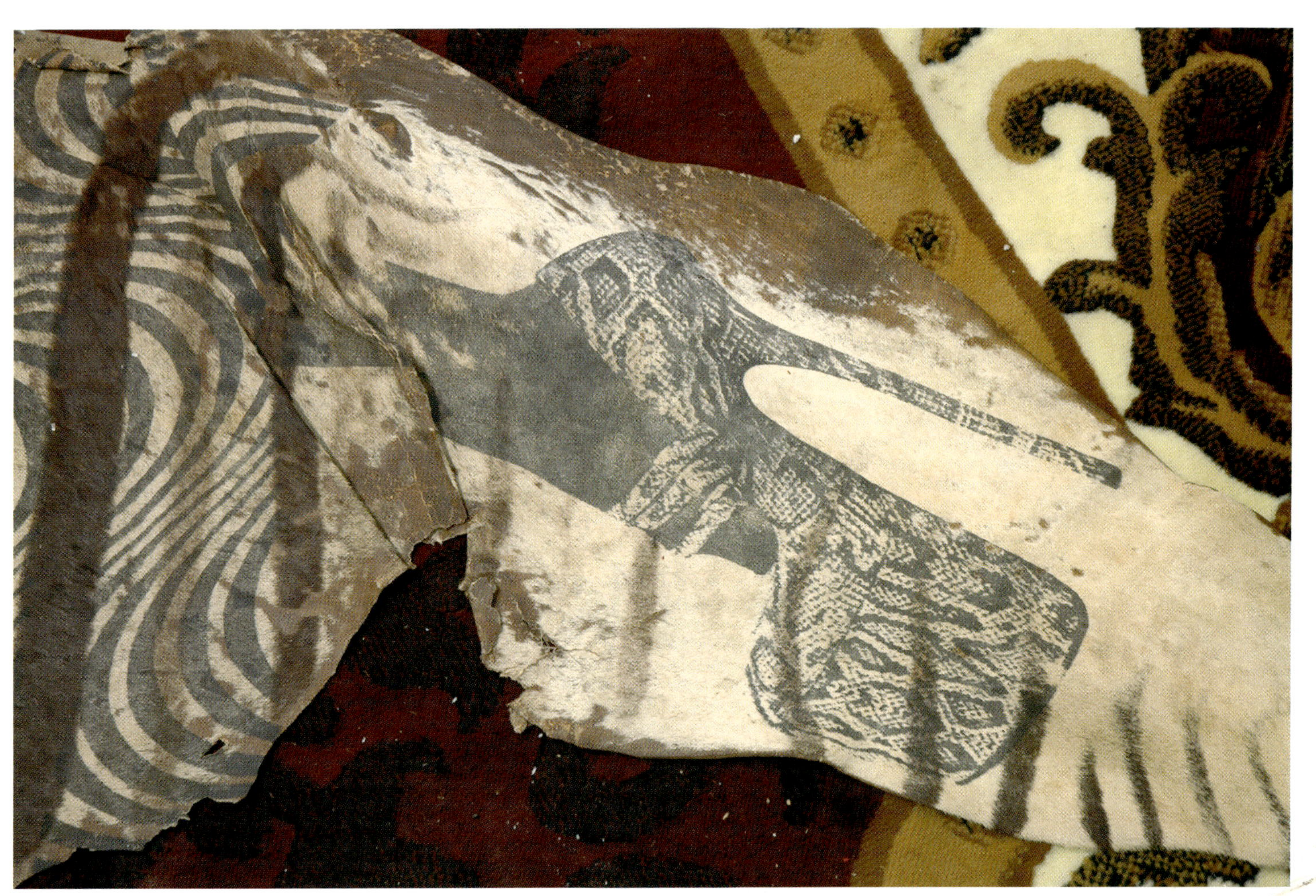

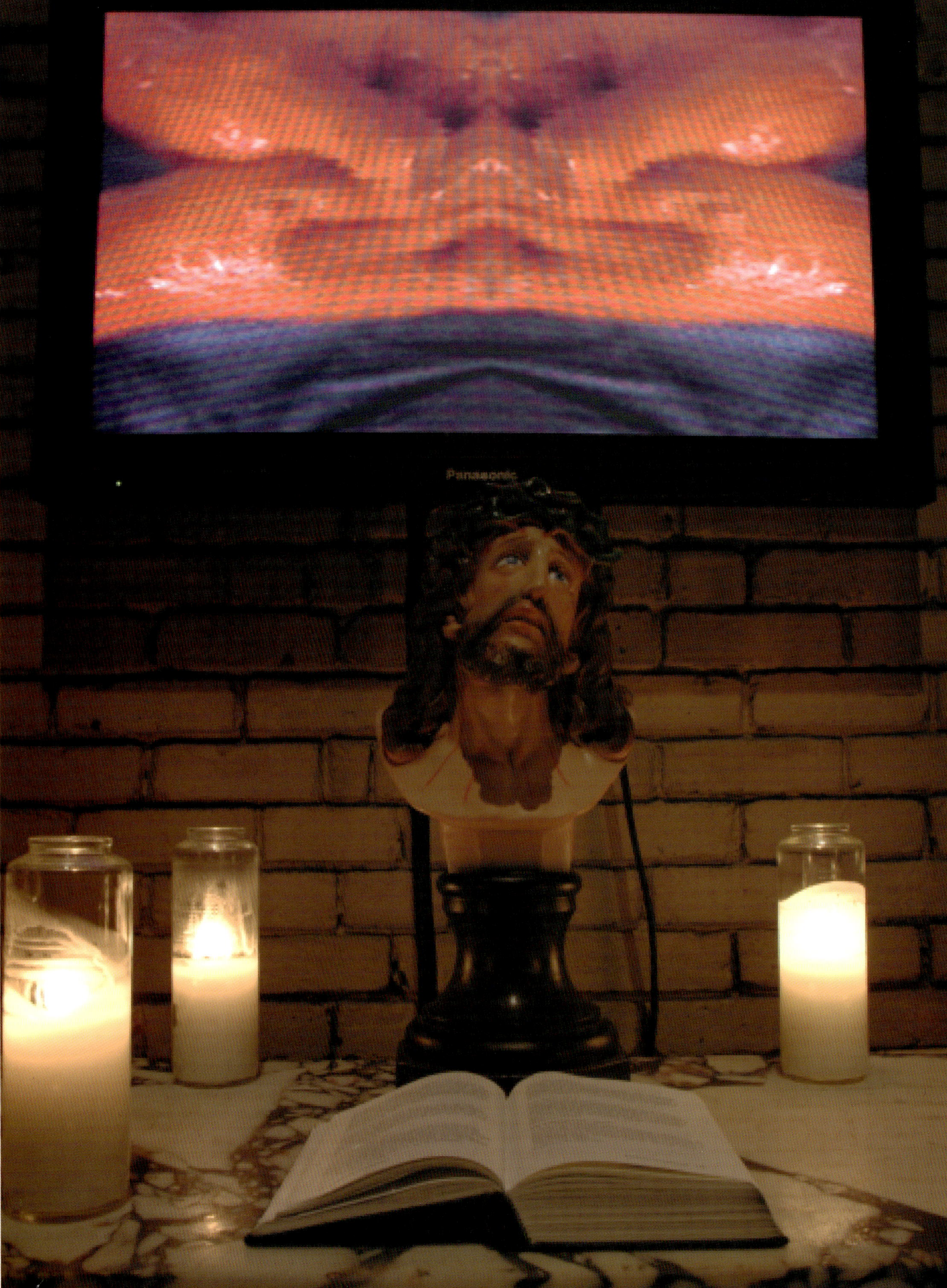

Panasonic

CHURCHILL MADIKIDA

Skeletons in My Closet
2004
Digital video, installed with found objects
DURATION 2 MIN 2 SEC
North Ambulatory, Cathedral of St John the Divine, 2004

Courtesy of the artist and Michael Stevenson Contemporary

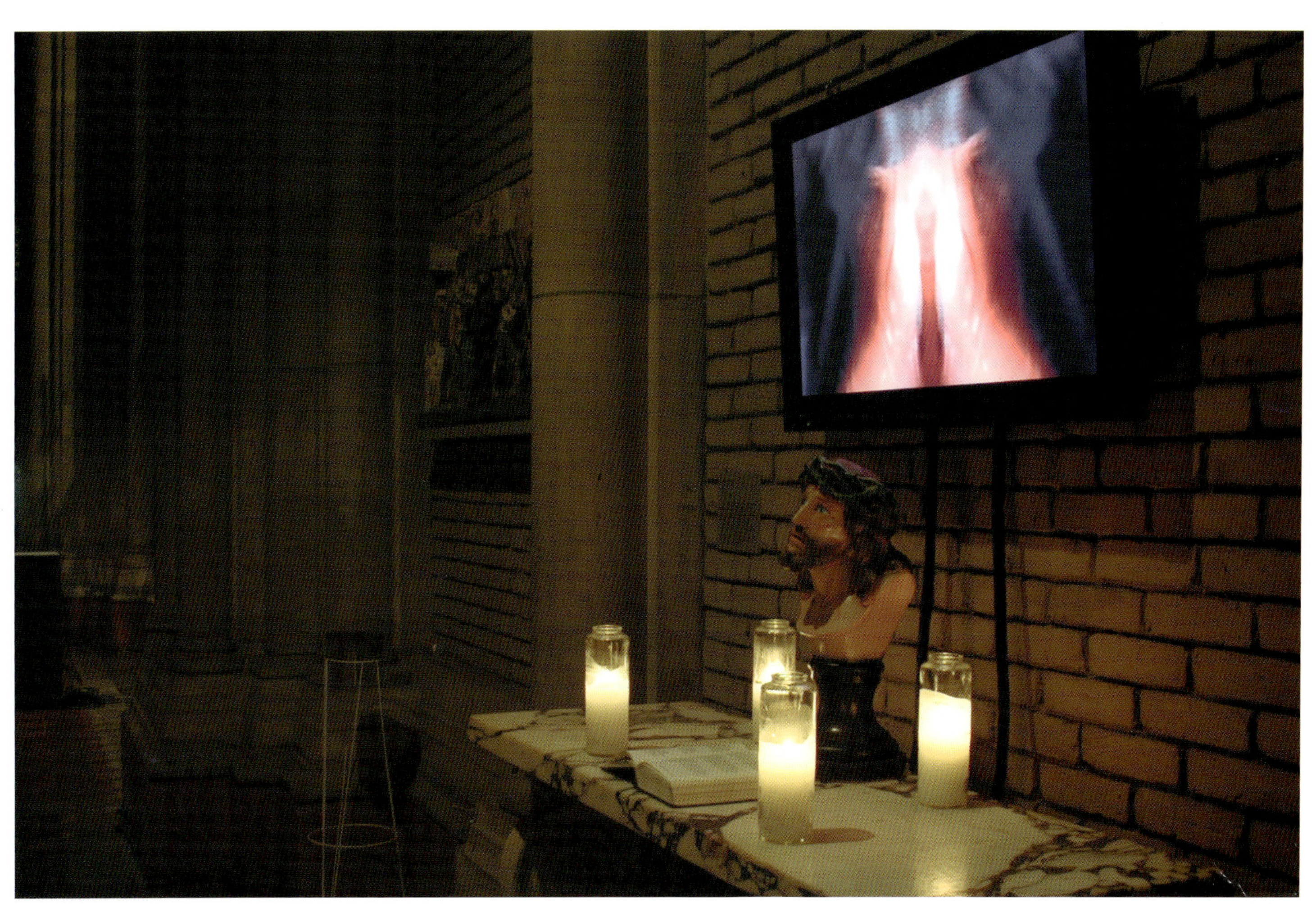

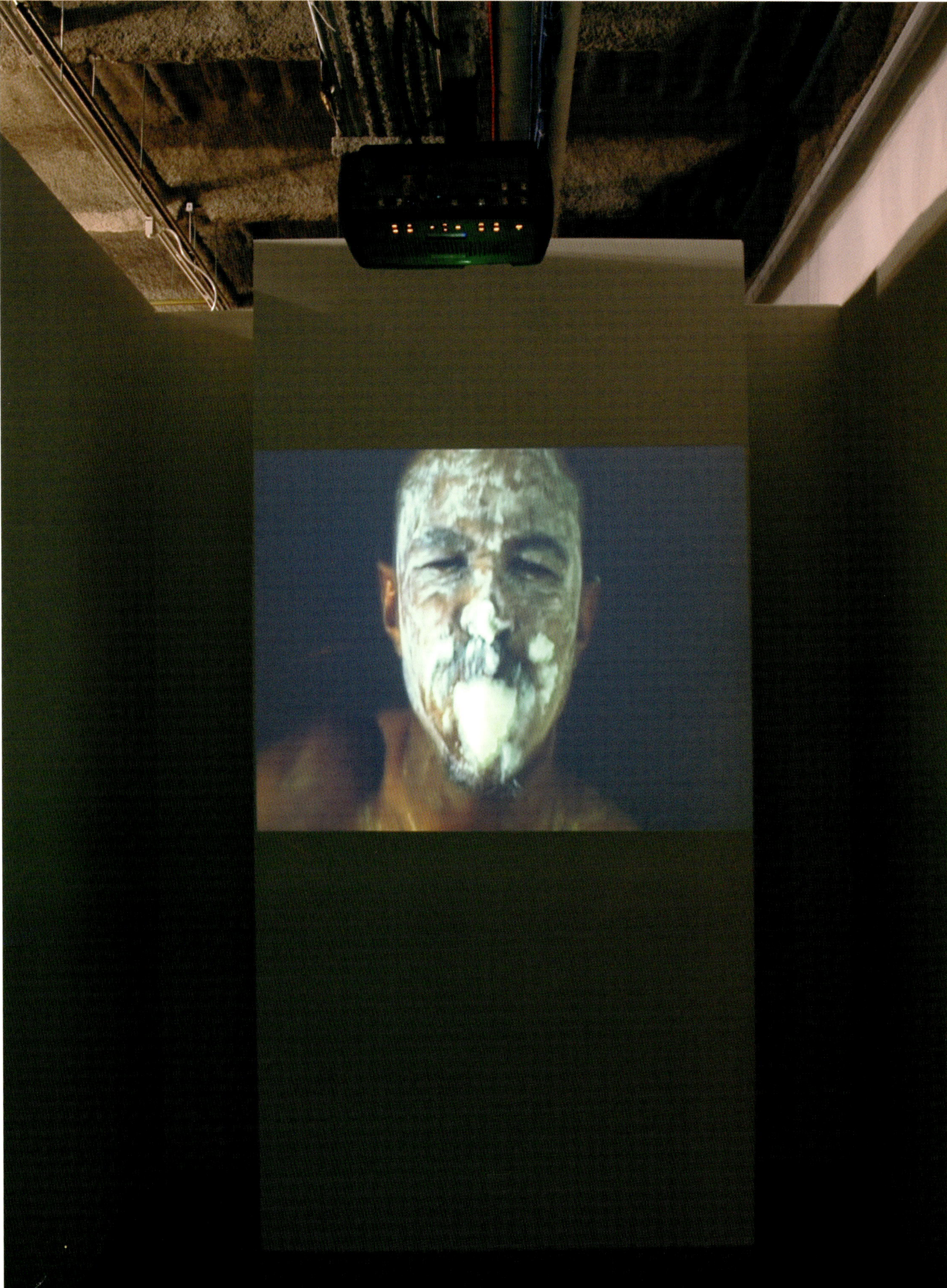

Struggles of the Heart
2003
Digital video
DURATION 2 MIN 54 SEC
Museum for African Art, 2004

Courtesy of the artist and Michael Stevenson Contemporary

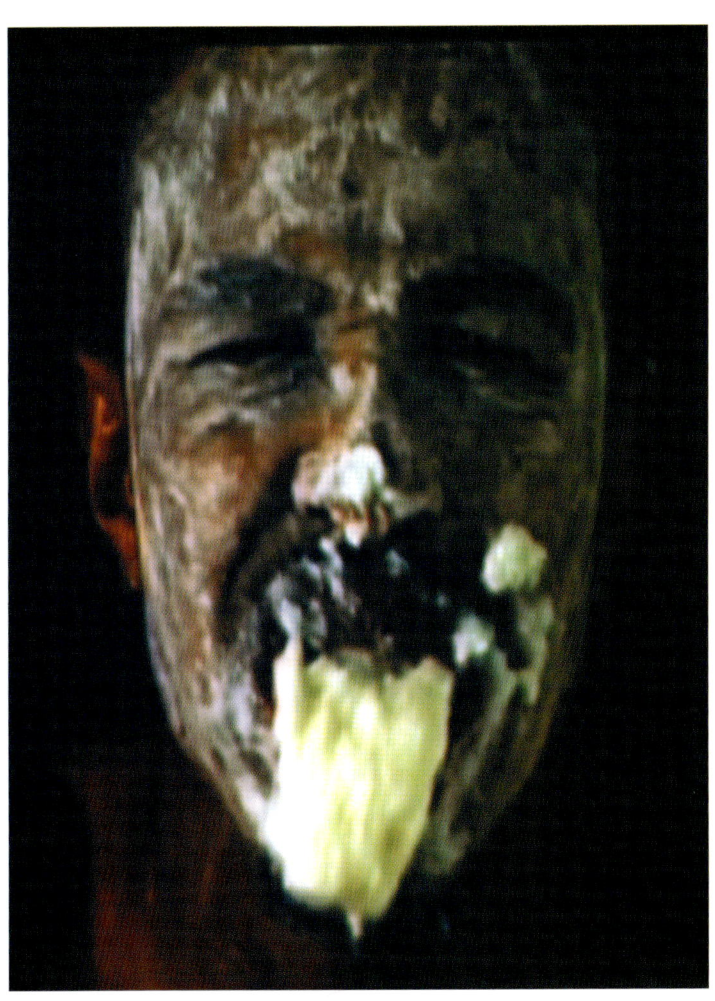
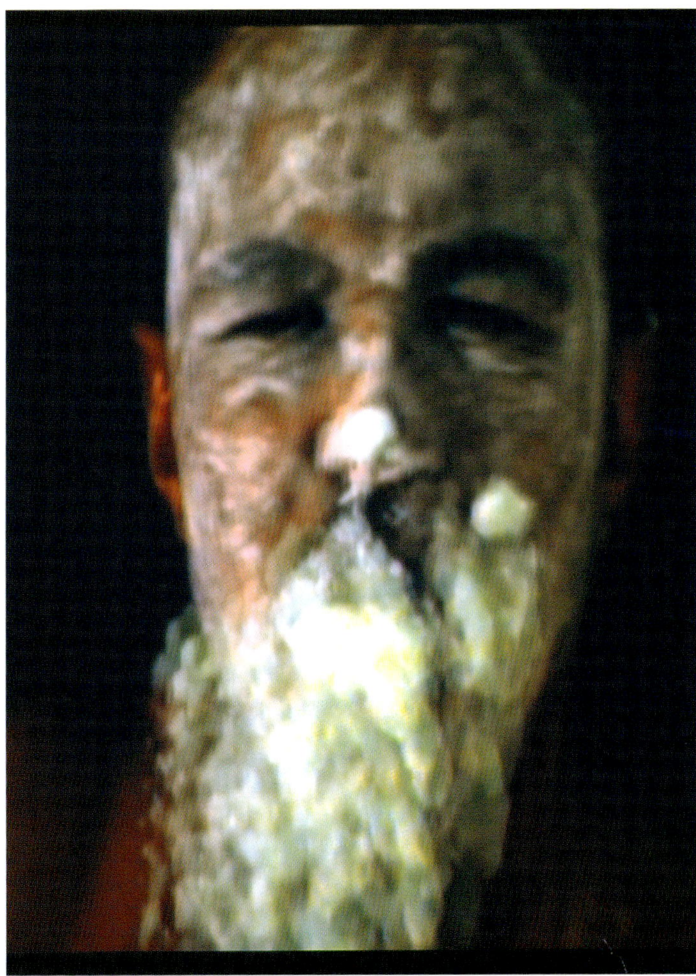

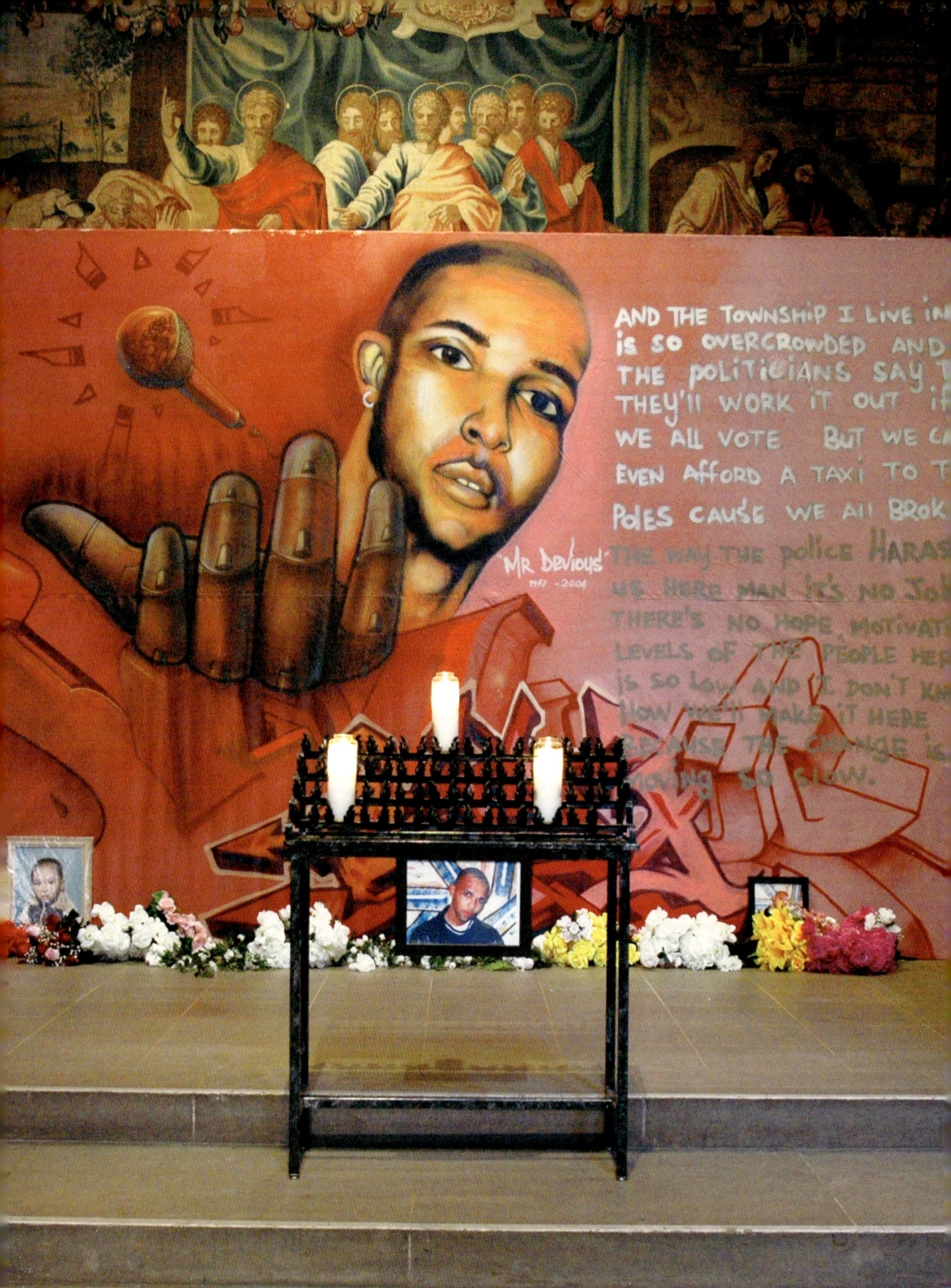
AND THE TOWNSHIP I LIVE IN
IS SO OVERCROWDED AND
THE POLITICIANS SAY T
THEY'LL WORK IT OUT IF
WE ALL VOTE BUT WE CA
EVEN AFFORD A TAXI TO T
POLES CAUSE WE ALL BROK
THE WAY THE POLICE HARAS
US HERE MAN IT'S NO JOK
THERE'S NO HOPE MOTIVAT
LEVELS OF THE PEOPLE HER
IS SO LOW AND I DON'T KN
HOW MUCH MAKE IT HERE
BECAUSE THE CHANGE IS
MOVING SO SLOW
"MR DEVIOUS"
1977 - 2004

MUSTAFA MALUKA

Tribute to Mr Devious
2004
Mixed media installation
DIMENSIONS VARIABLE
Crusaders Bay, Cathedral of St John the Divine, 2004

Commissioned by *Season South Africa* for *Personal Affects*
Courtesy of the artist

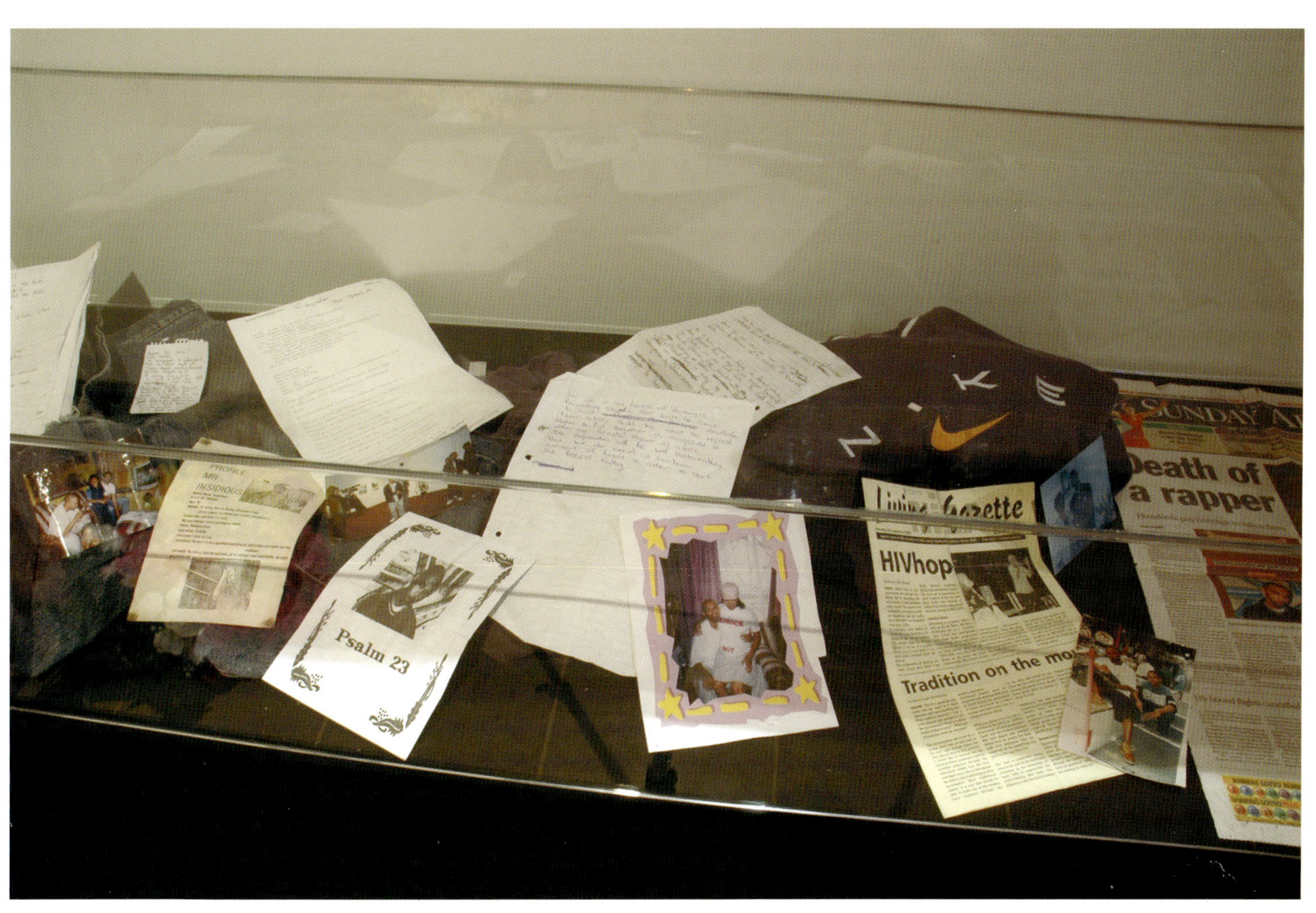

The Realness
2002
Mixed media on canvas
183 X 133 CM
Museum for African Art, 2004

Courtesy of the artist

Soul on Ice
2002
Acrylic and oil on canvas
183 X 133 CM
Museum for African Art, 2004

Courtesy of the artist

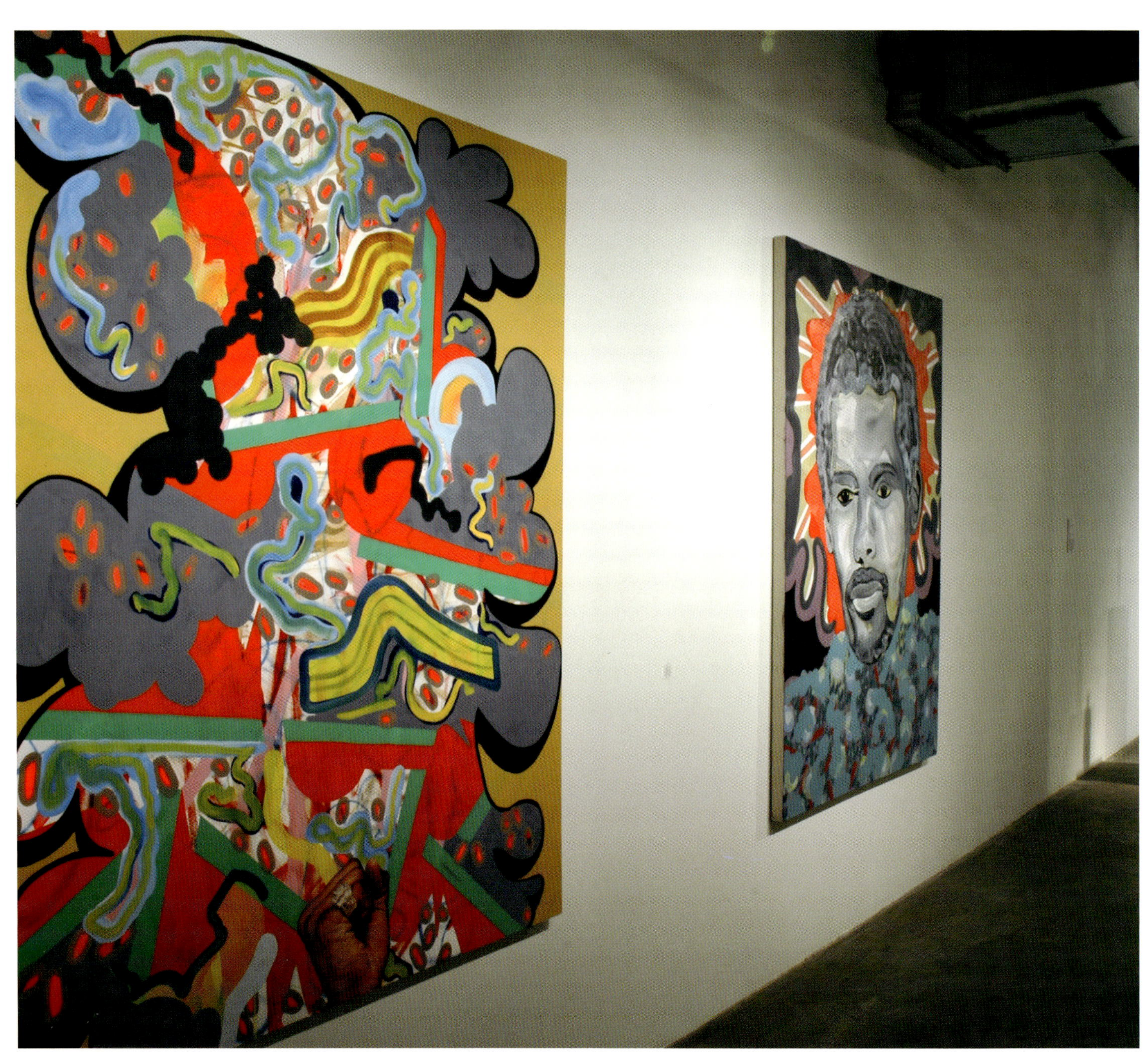

Seen It All
2002
Acrylic and oil on canvas
183 X 133 CM
Museum for African Art, 2004

Courtesy of the artist

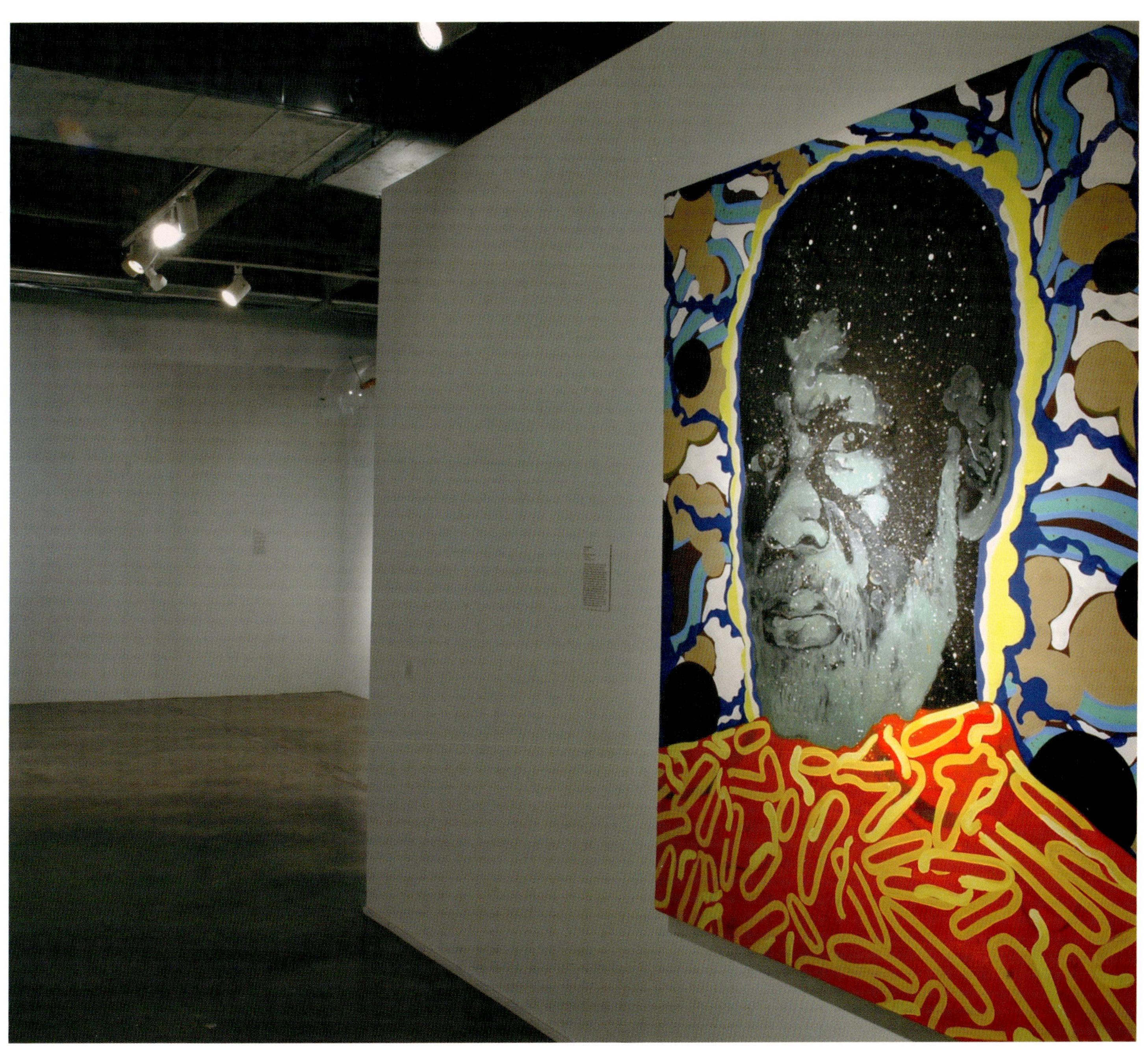

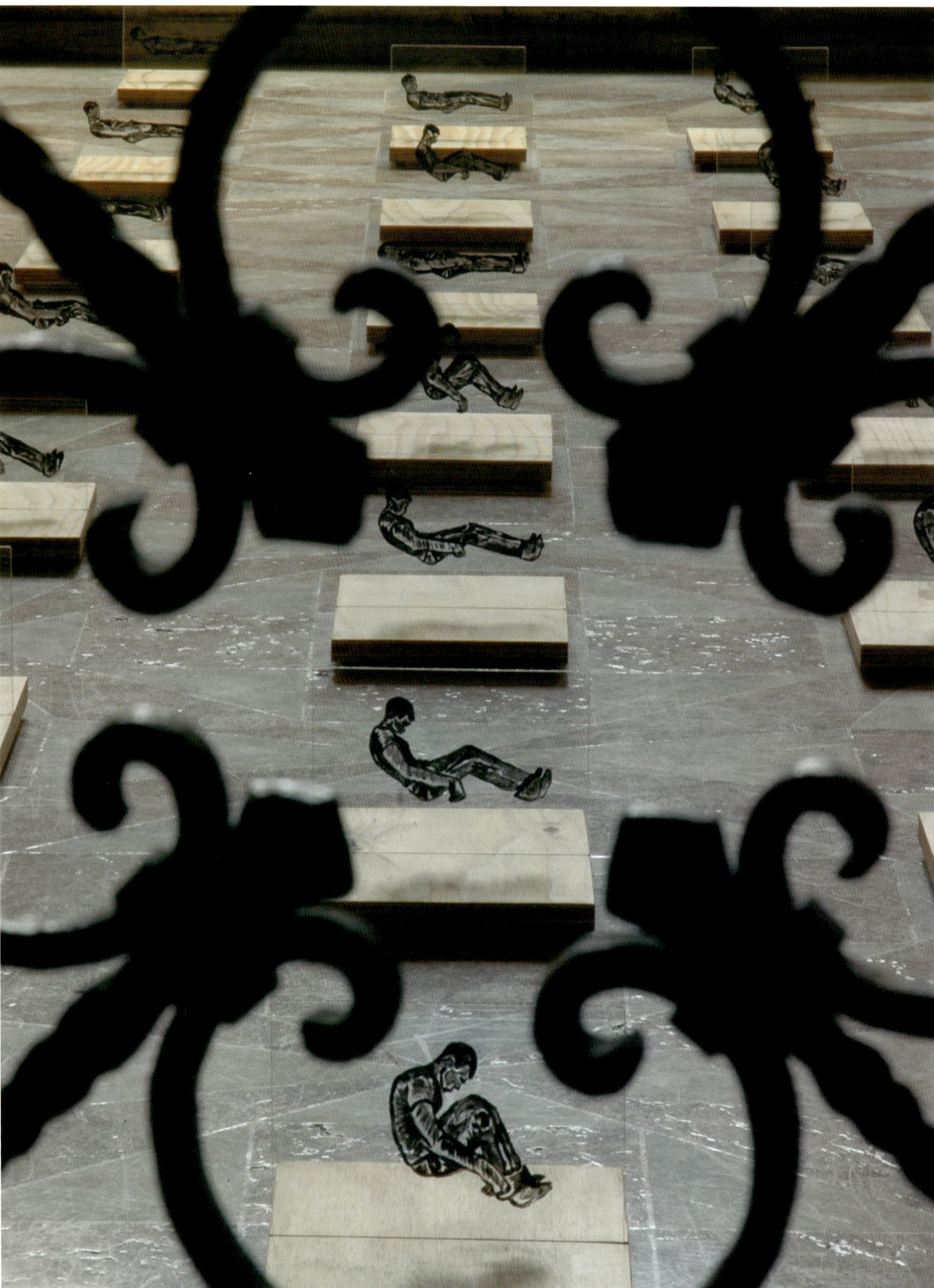

THANDO MAMA

1994 (II)
2004
Mixed media installation
DIMENSIONS VARIABLE
Chapel of St Ambrose, Cathedral of St John the Divine, 2004

Commissioned by *Season South Africa* for *Personal Affects*
Courtesy of the artist

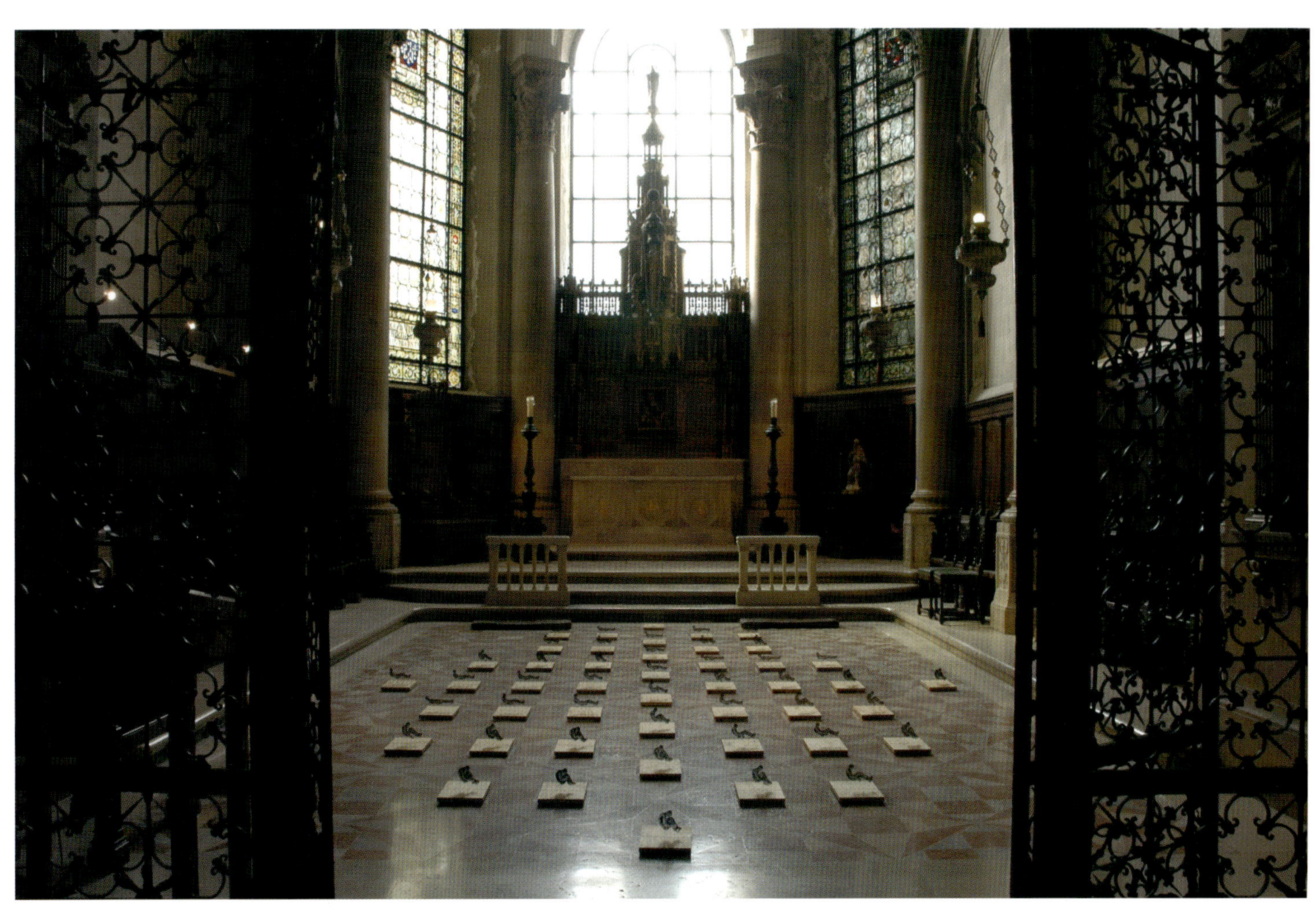

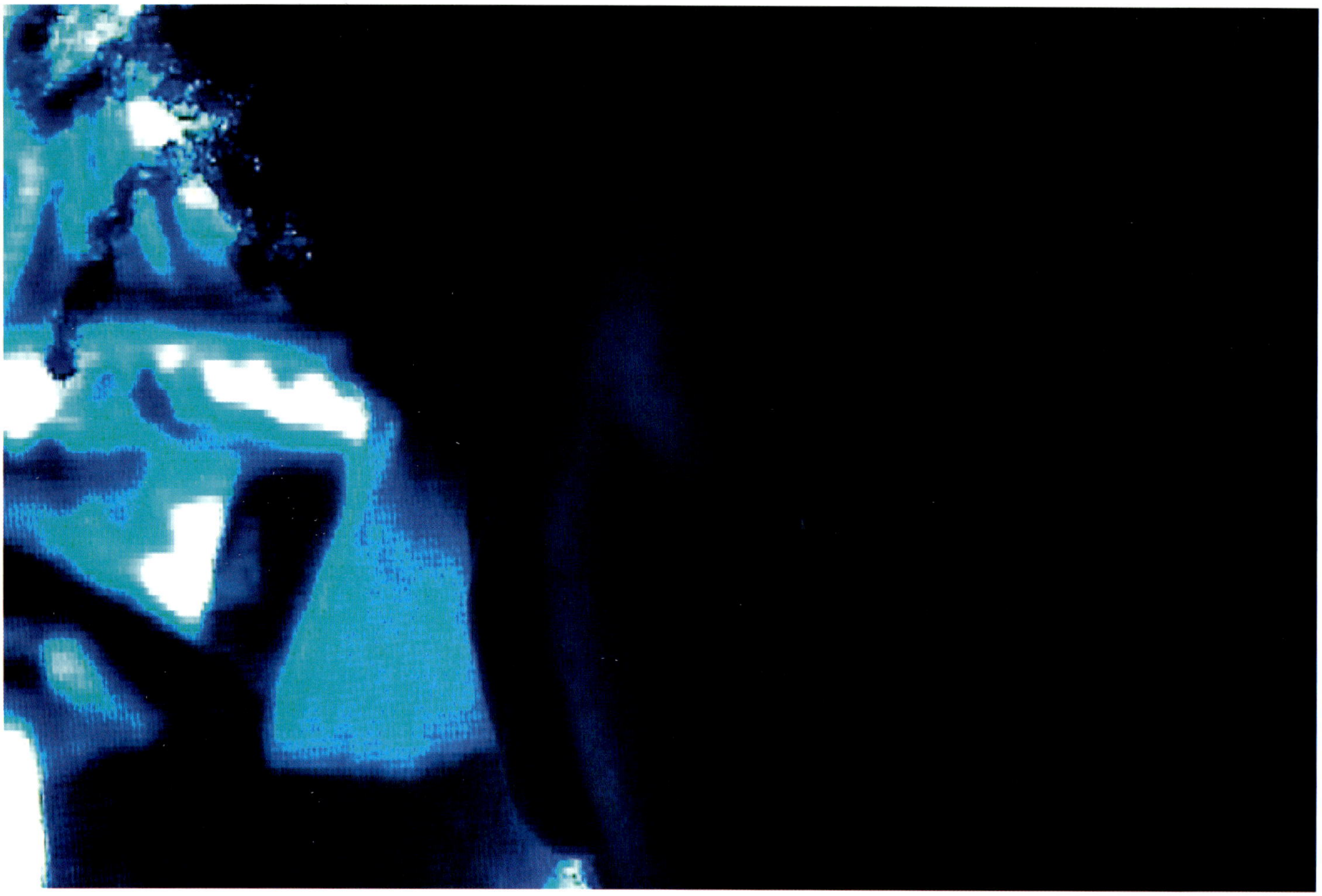

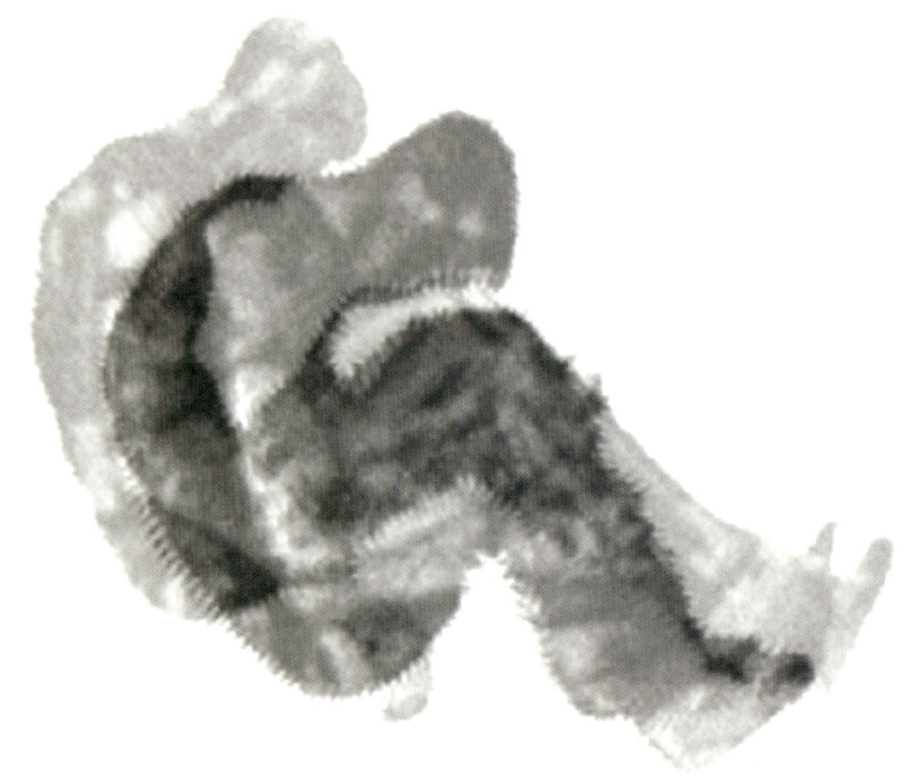

1994 (I)
2004
Mixed media installation with twin video projections
DURATION 1 MIN 55 SEC EACH
Museum for African Art, 2004

Commissioned by *Season South Africa* for *Personal Affects*
Courtesy of the artist

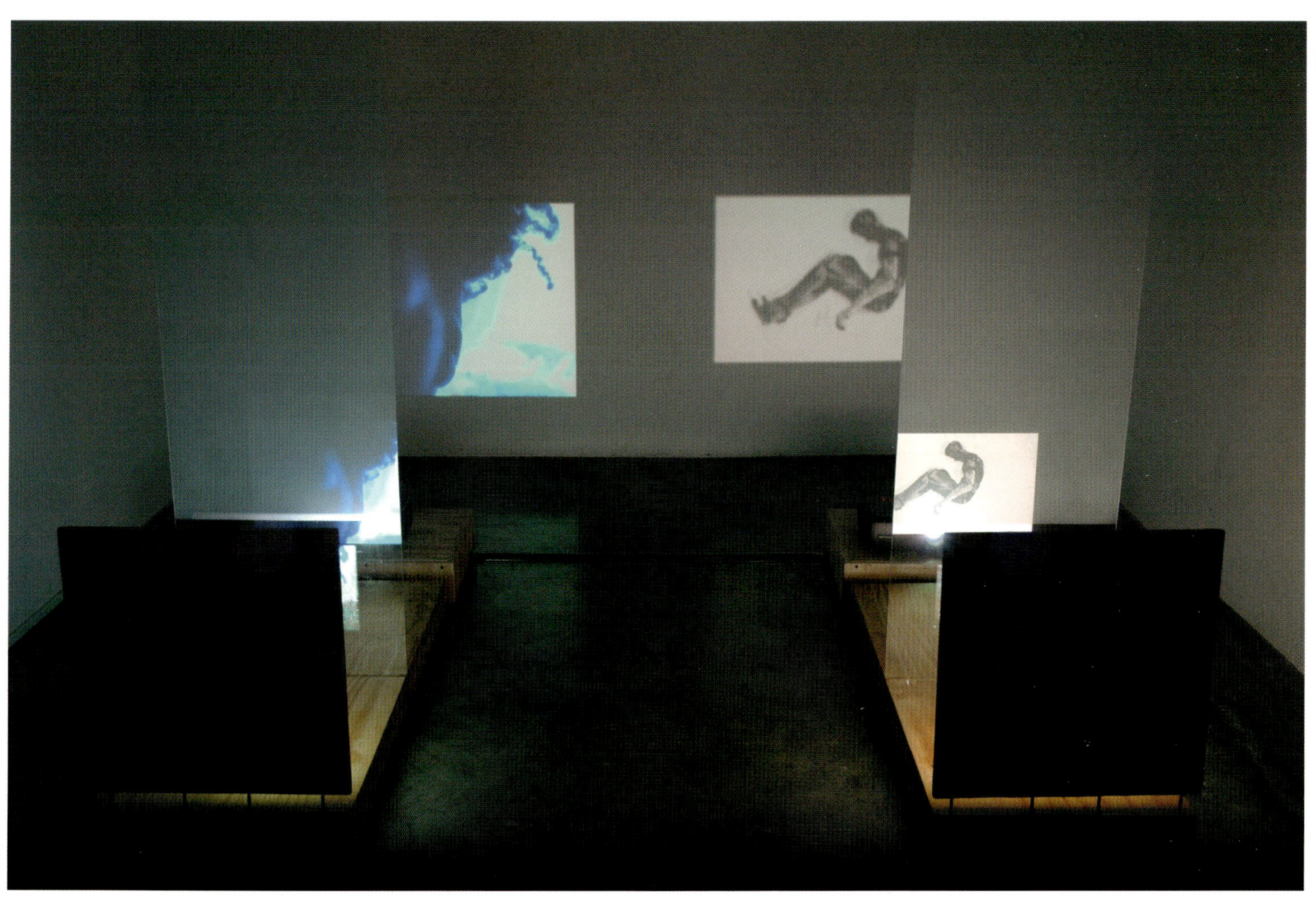

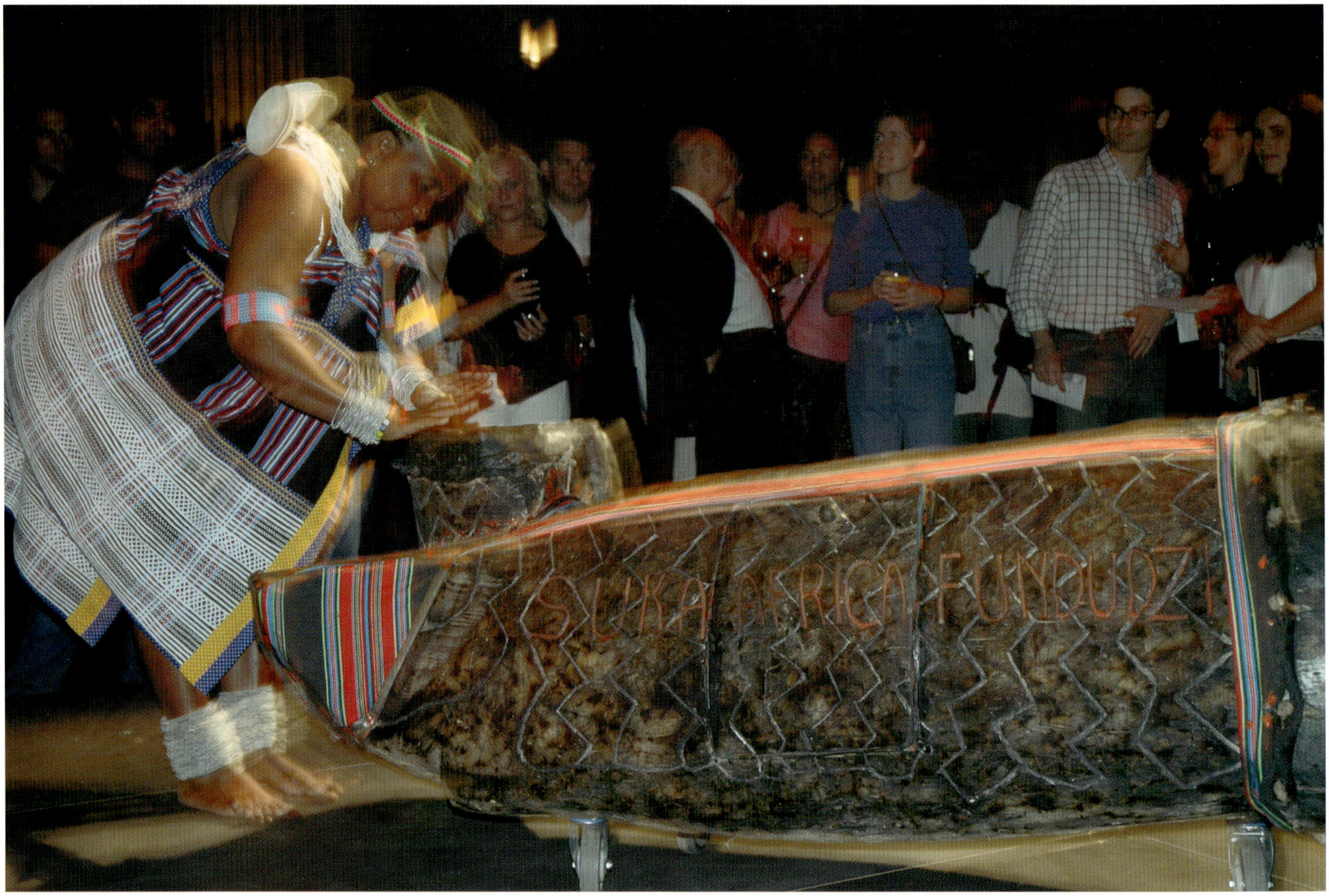

SUKA AFRICA FUNDUDZI

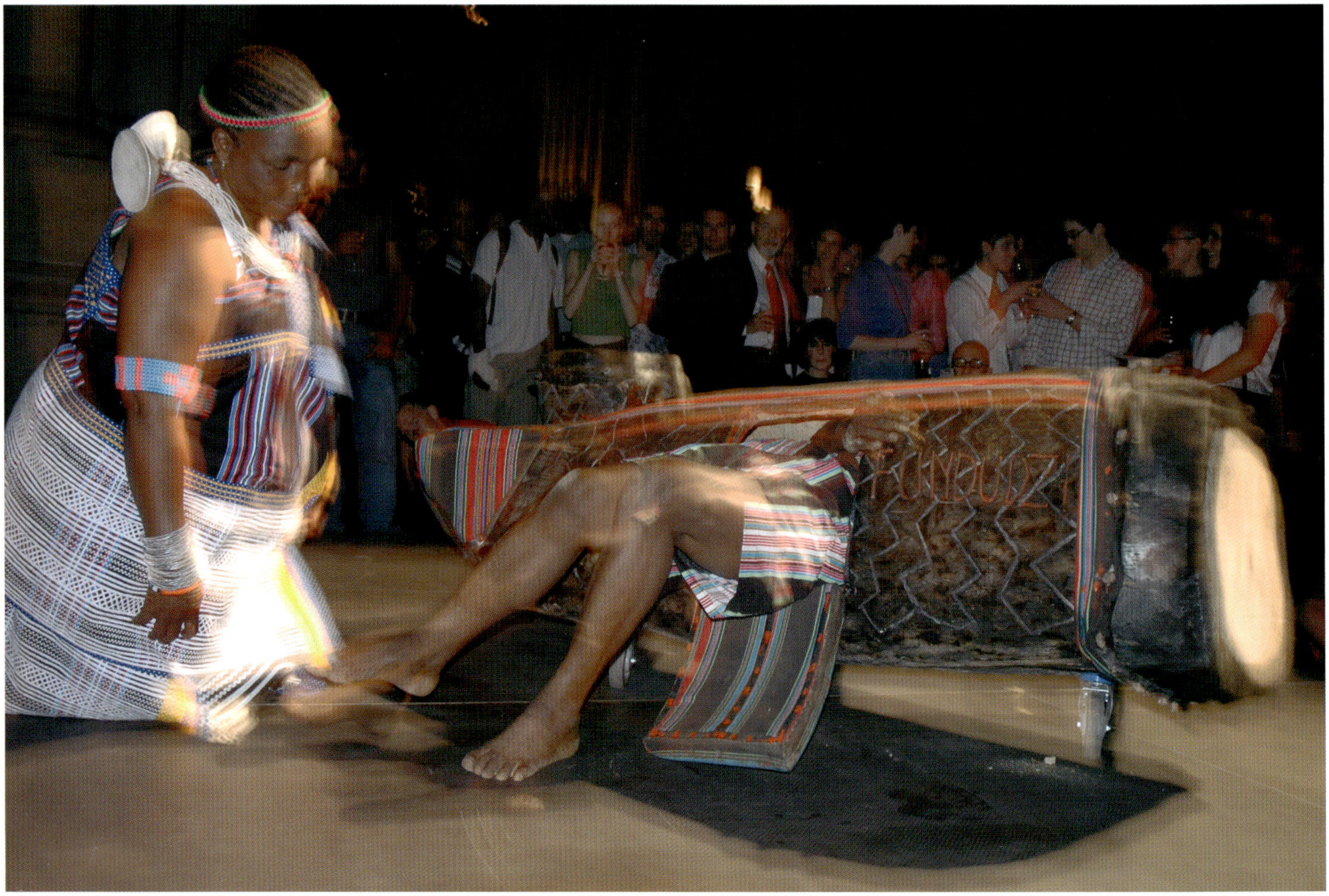

FUNDUDZI

SAMSON MUDZUNGA

Suka Africa Fundudzi
2004
Performance with drum: wood, enamel paint, animal hide
DRUM 150 X 300 X 100 CM
The Nave, Cathedral of St John the Divine, 23 September 2004

Commissioned by *Season South Africa* for *Personal Affects*
Courtesy of the artist and Michael Stevenson Contemporary

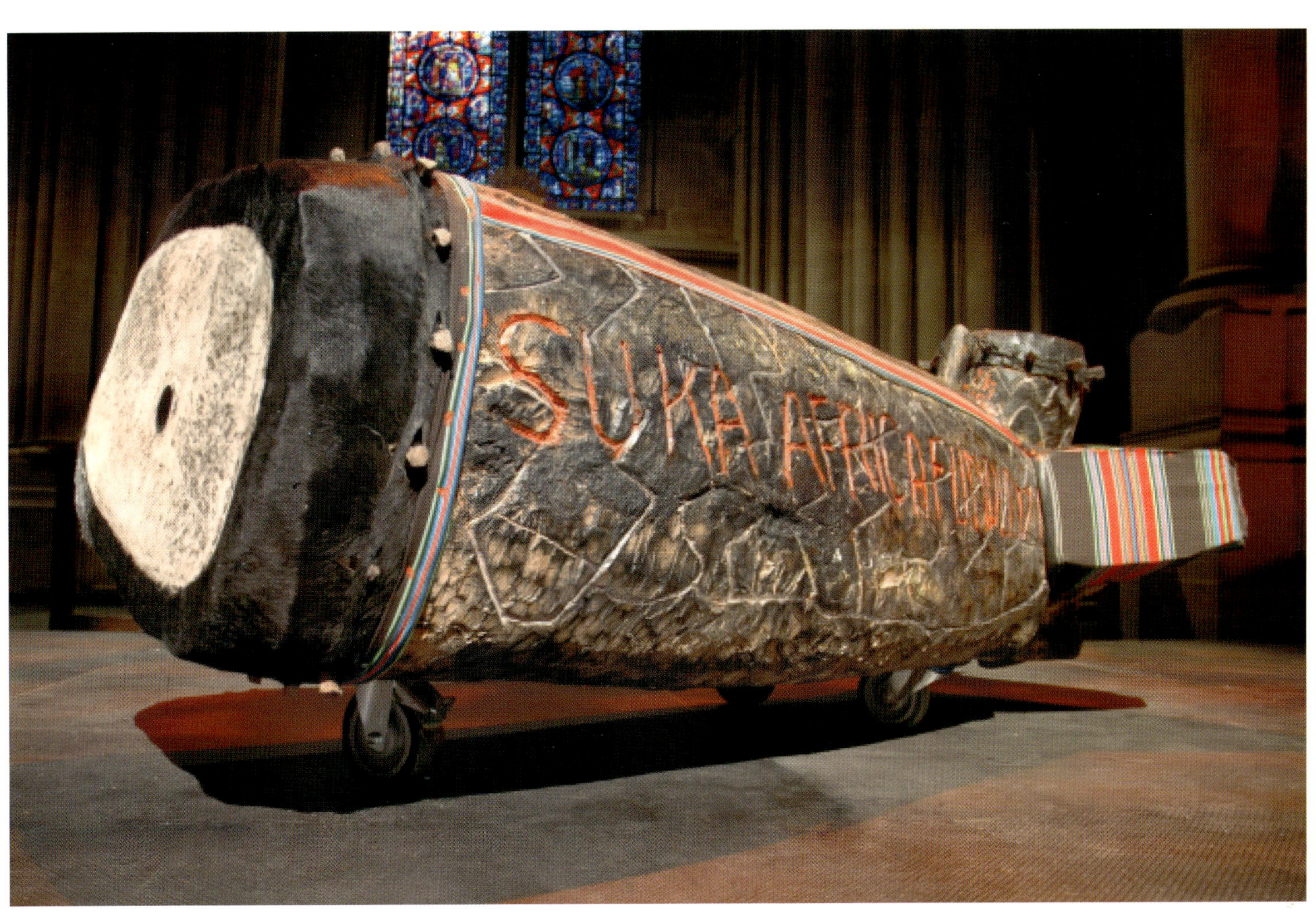

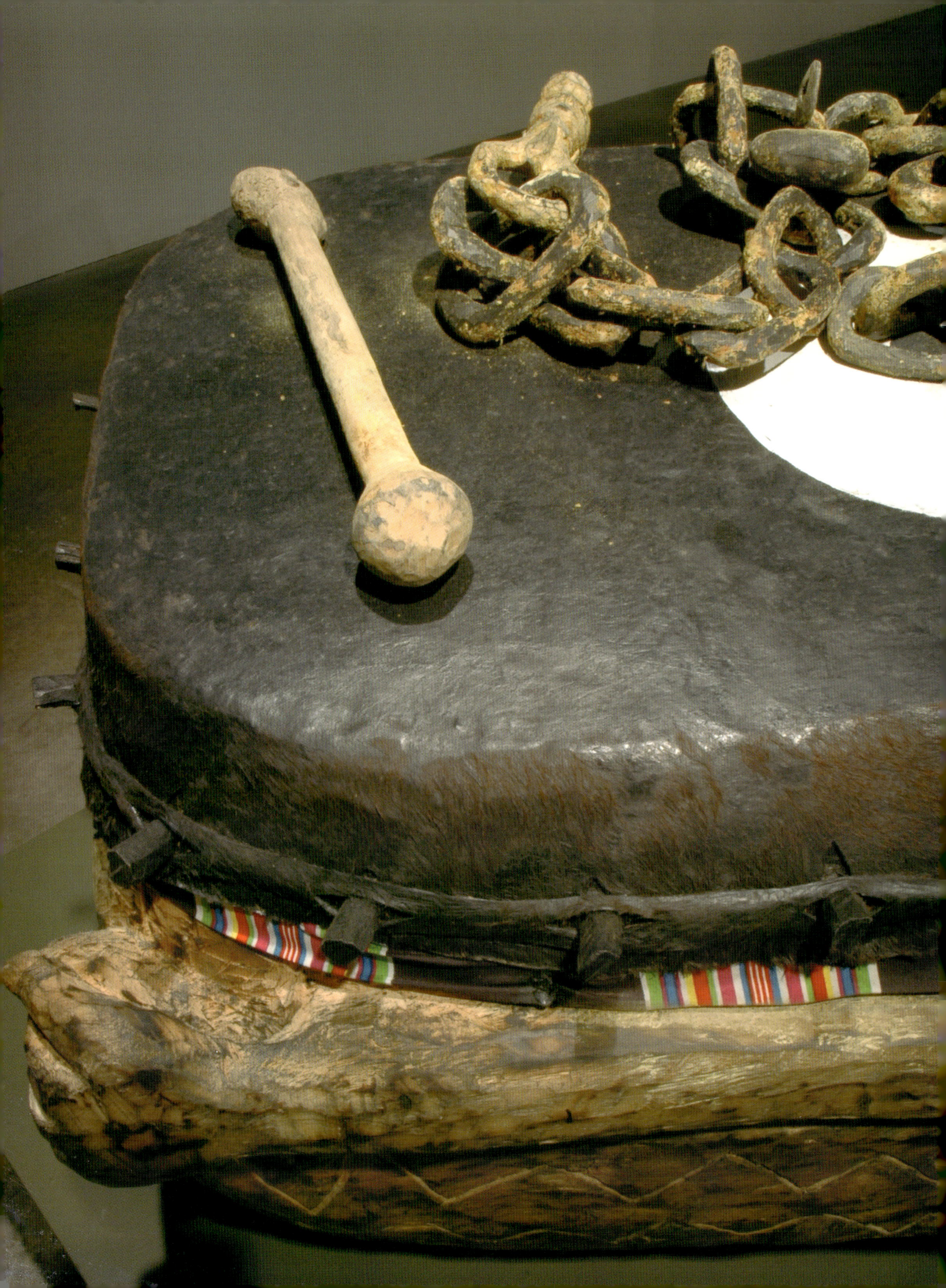

Suka Africa Fundudzi
2004
Wood, enamel paint, animal hide, video by John Hodgkiss
DRUM 102 X 68 X 75 CM
Museum for African Art, 2004

Commissioned by *Season South Africa* for *Personal Affects*
Courtesy of the artist and Michael Stevenson Contemporary

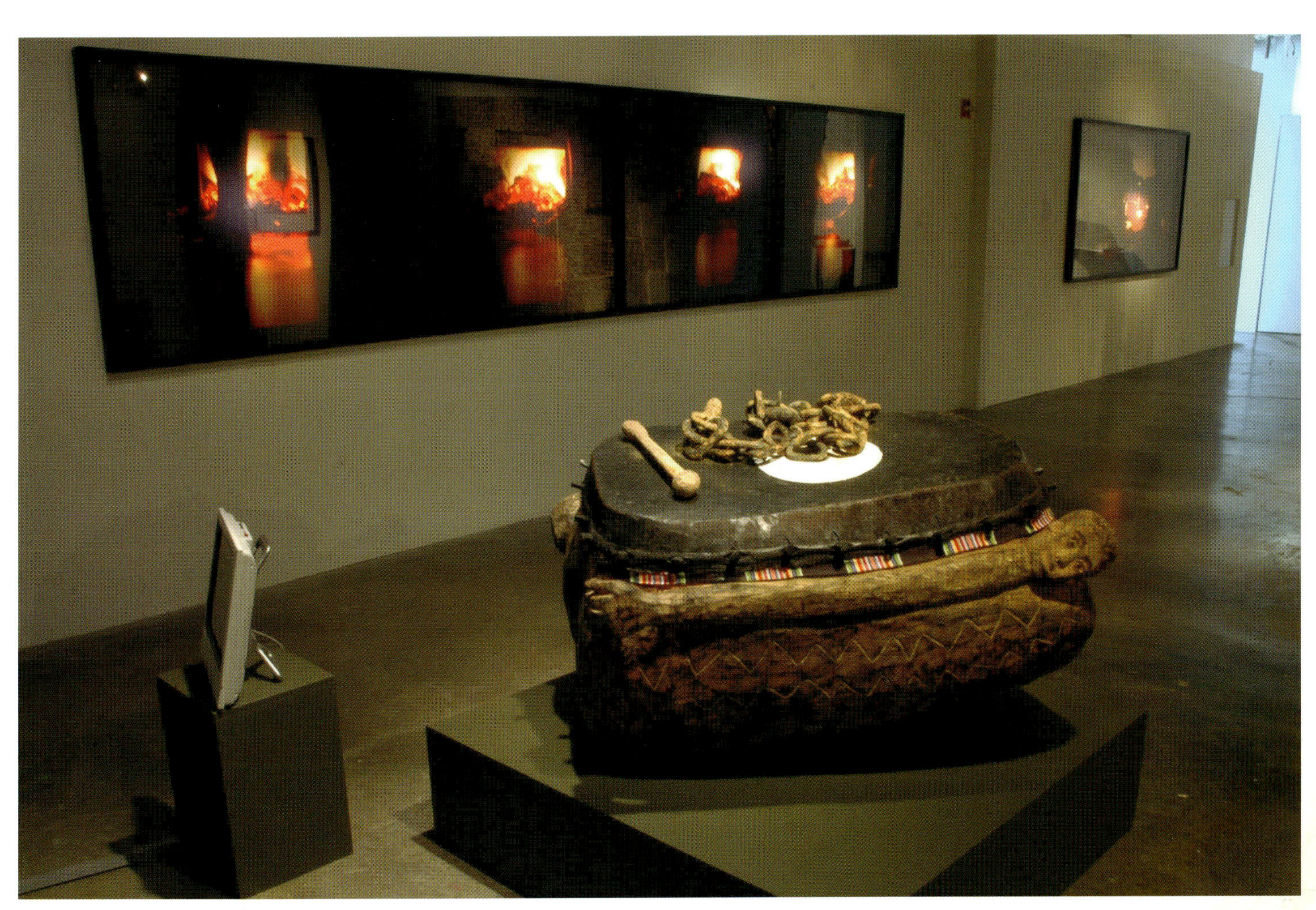

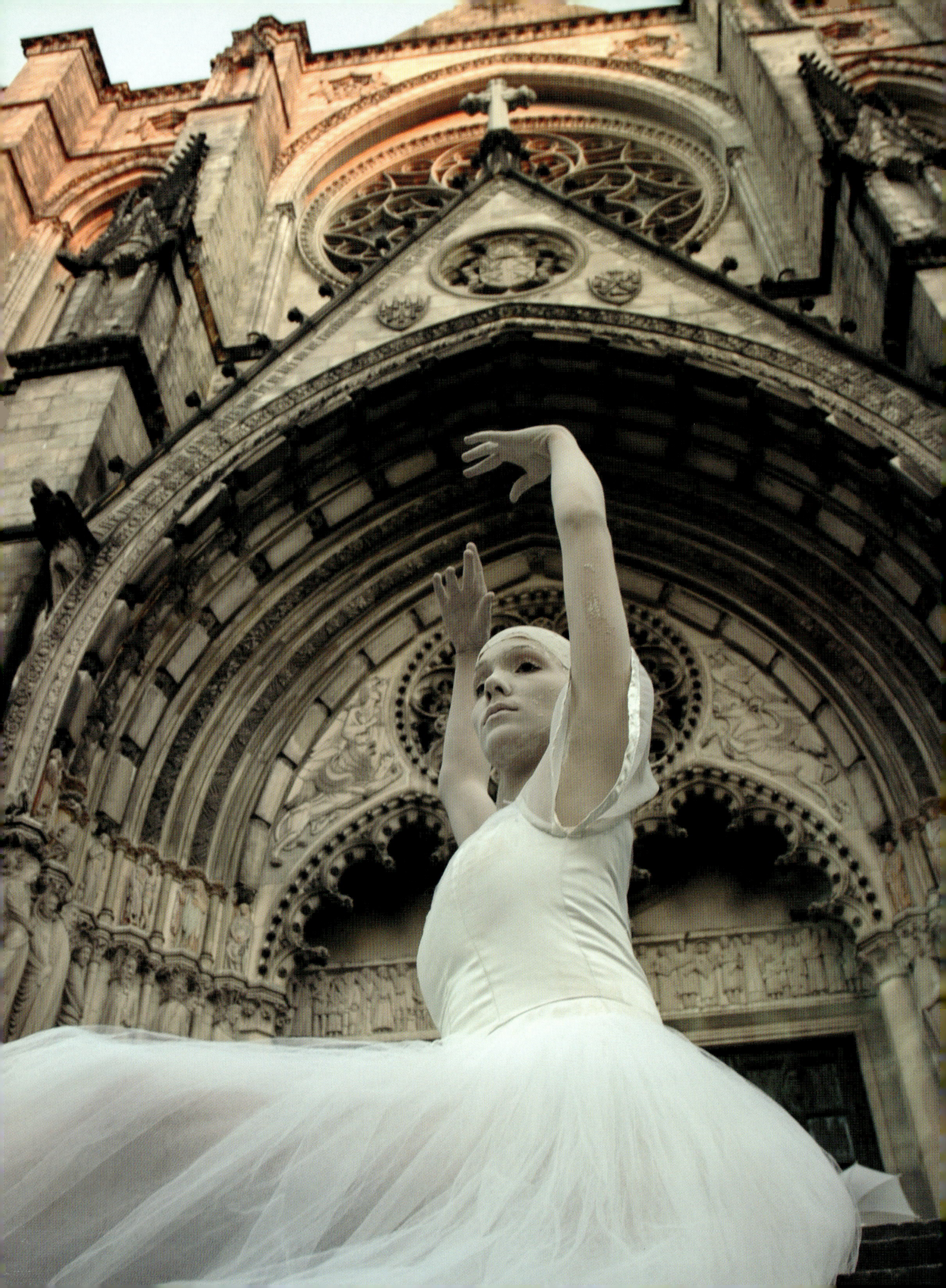

JAY PATHER

these pages and overleaf
From Before
2003–2004
Performance with 24 dancers
DURATION 17 MINS
Front steps, Cathedral of St John the Divine, 23 September 2004

Courtesy of the artist

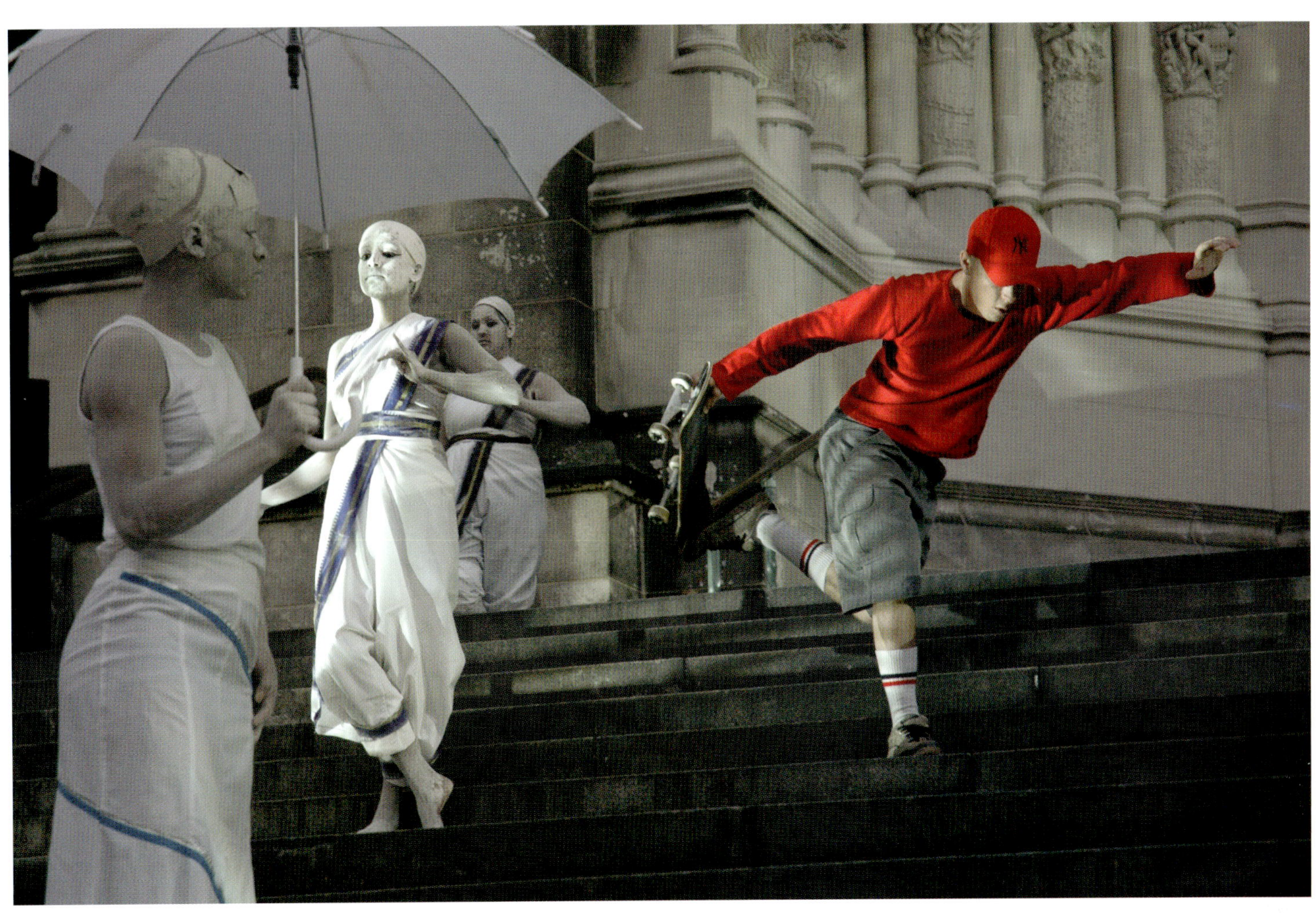

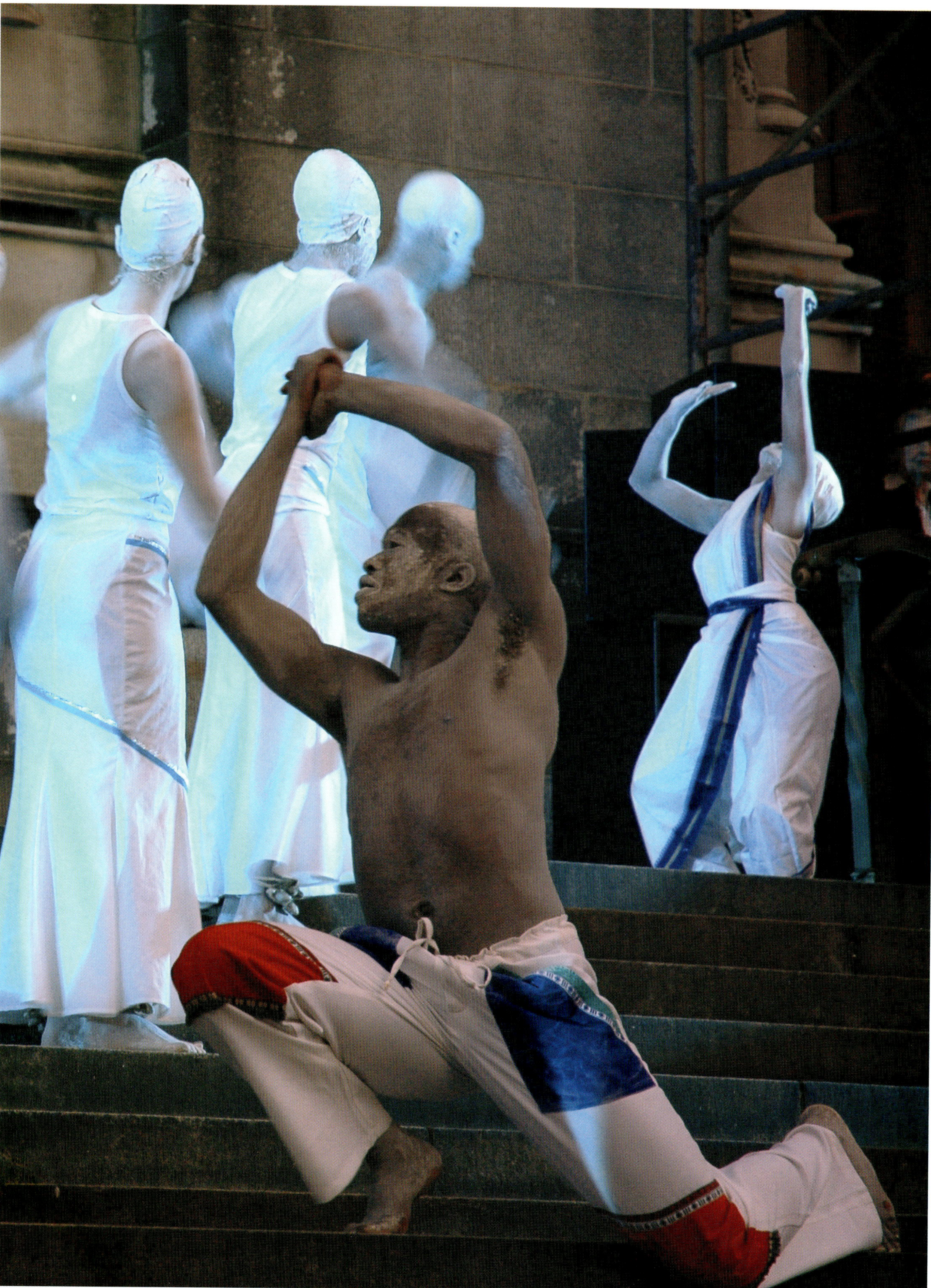

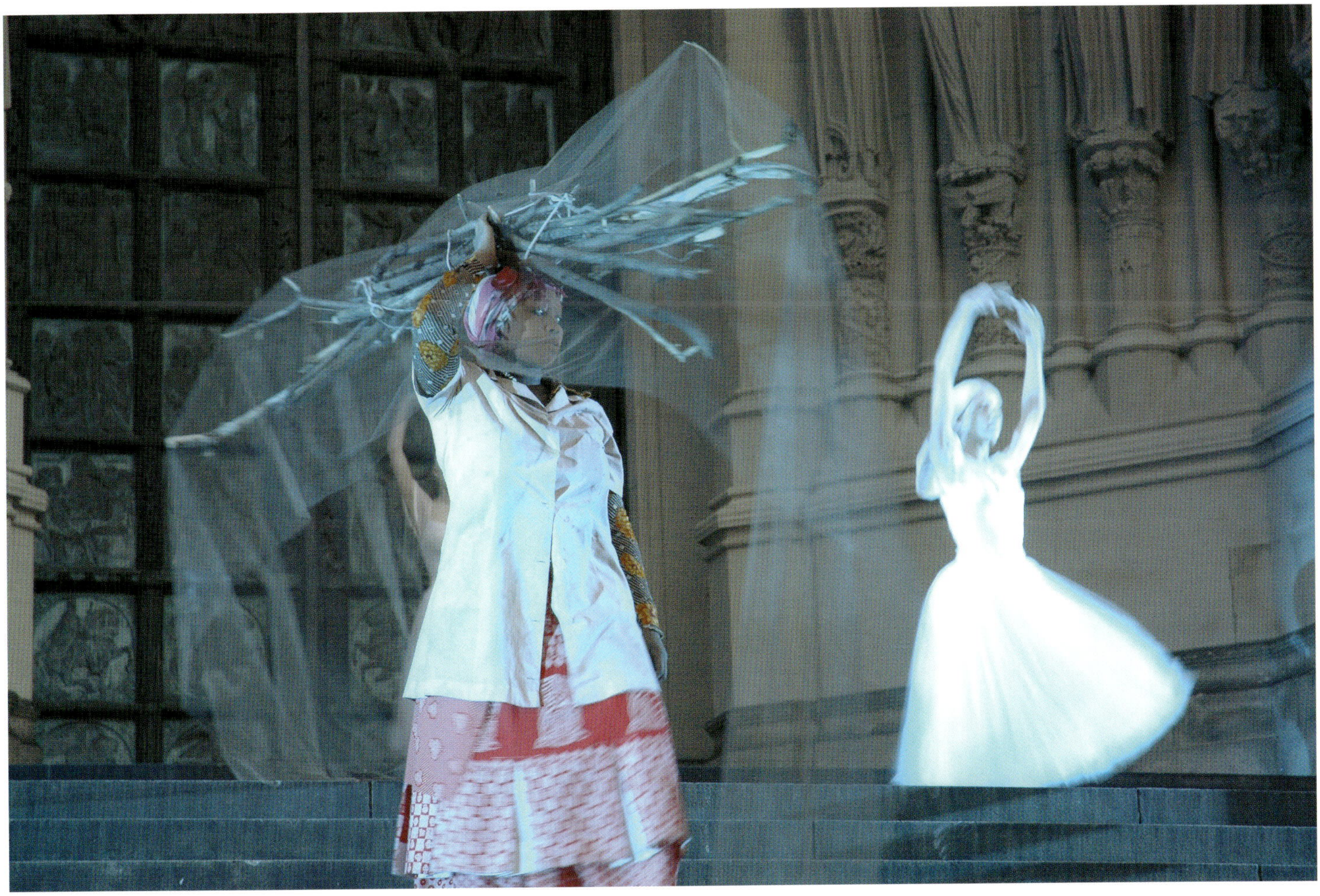

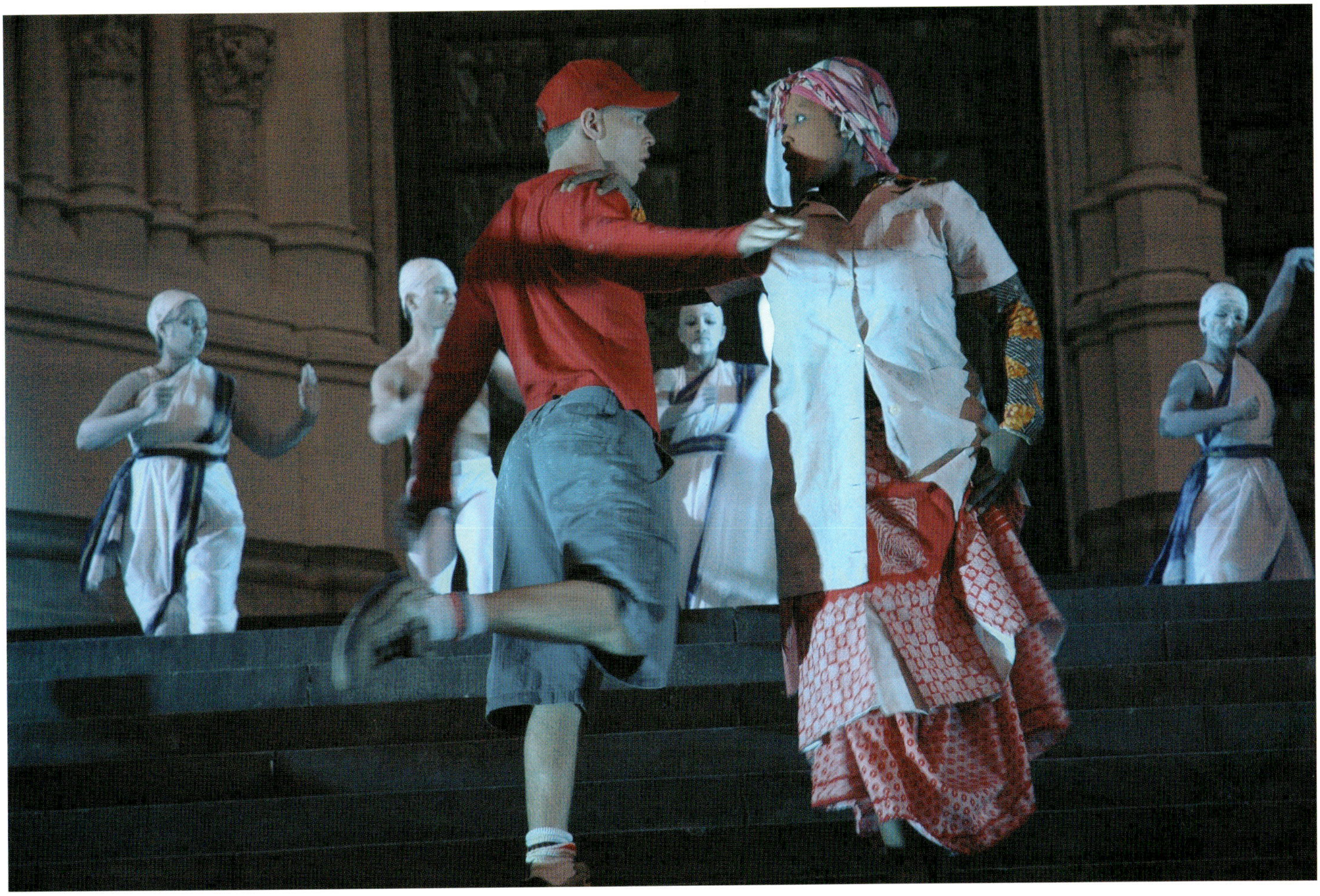

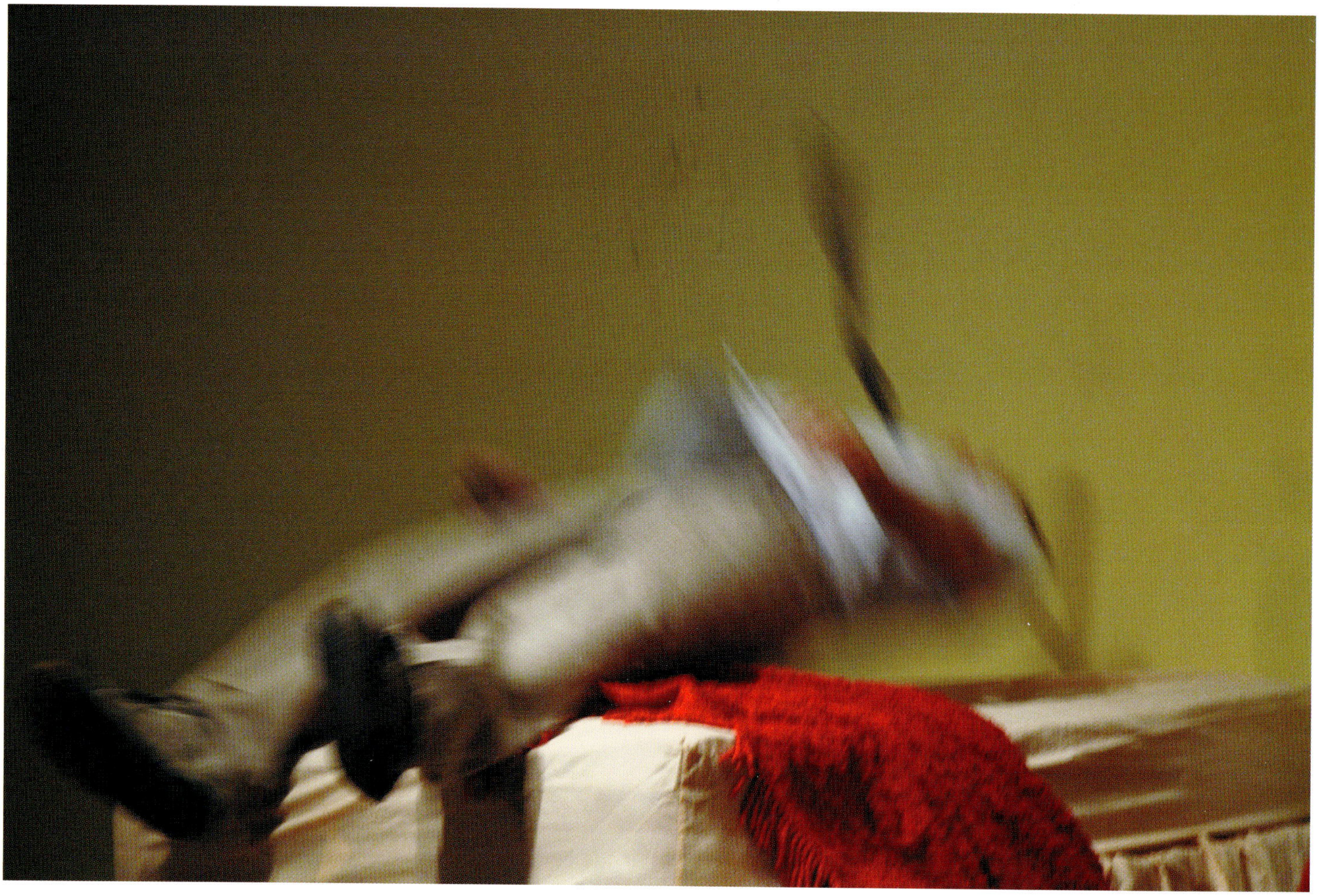

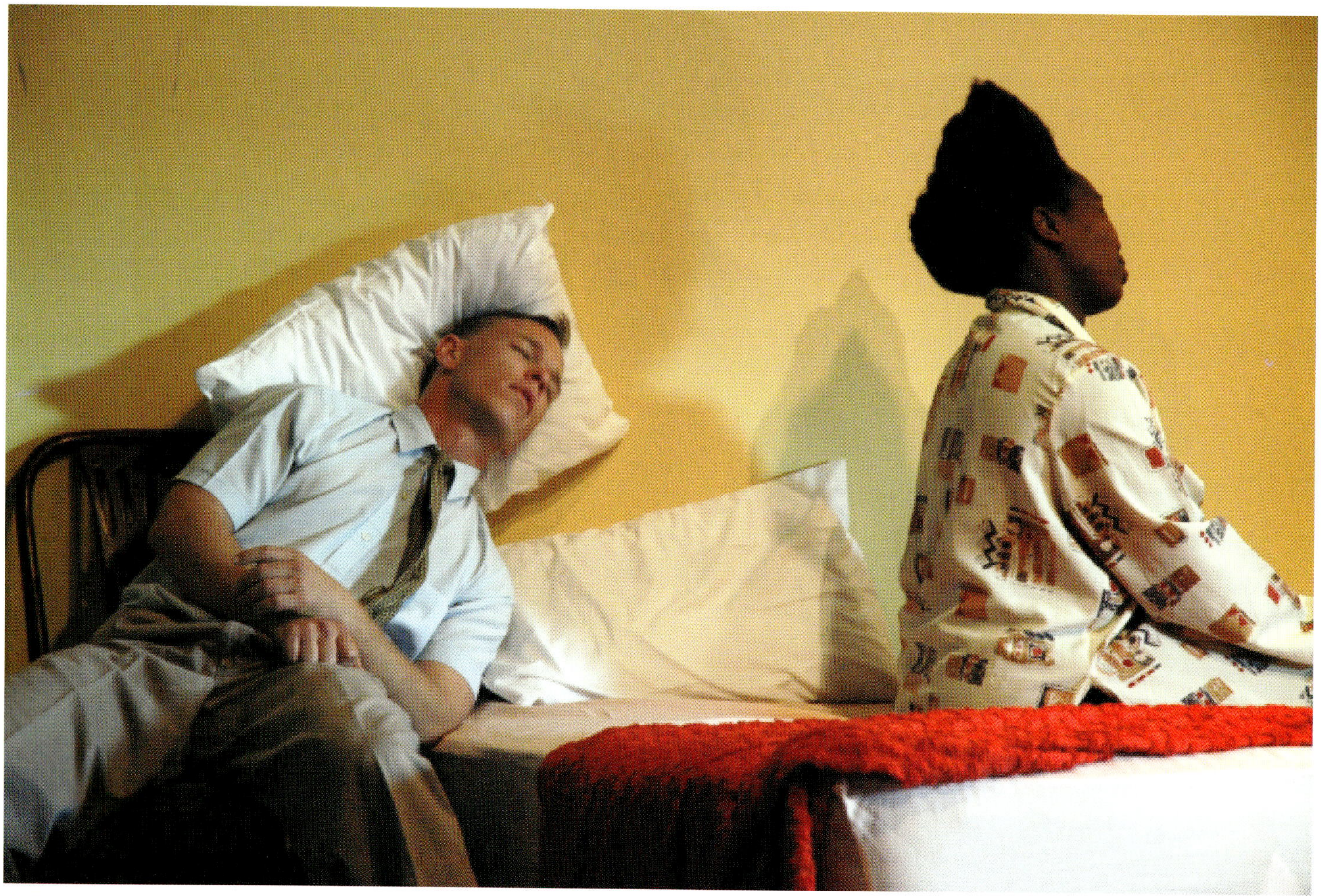

Hotel
2003–2004
Performance with three dancers:
Ntombi Gasa, Denton Douglas and Sifiso Majola
DURATION 20 MINS
Museum for African Art, 21 and 26 September 2004

Courtesy of the artist

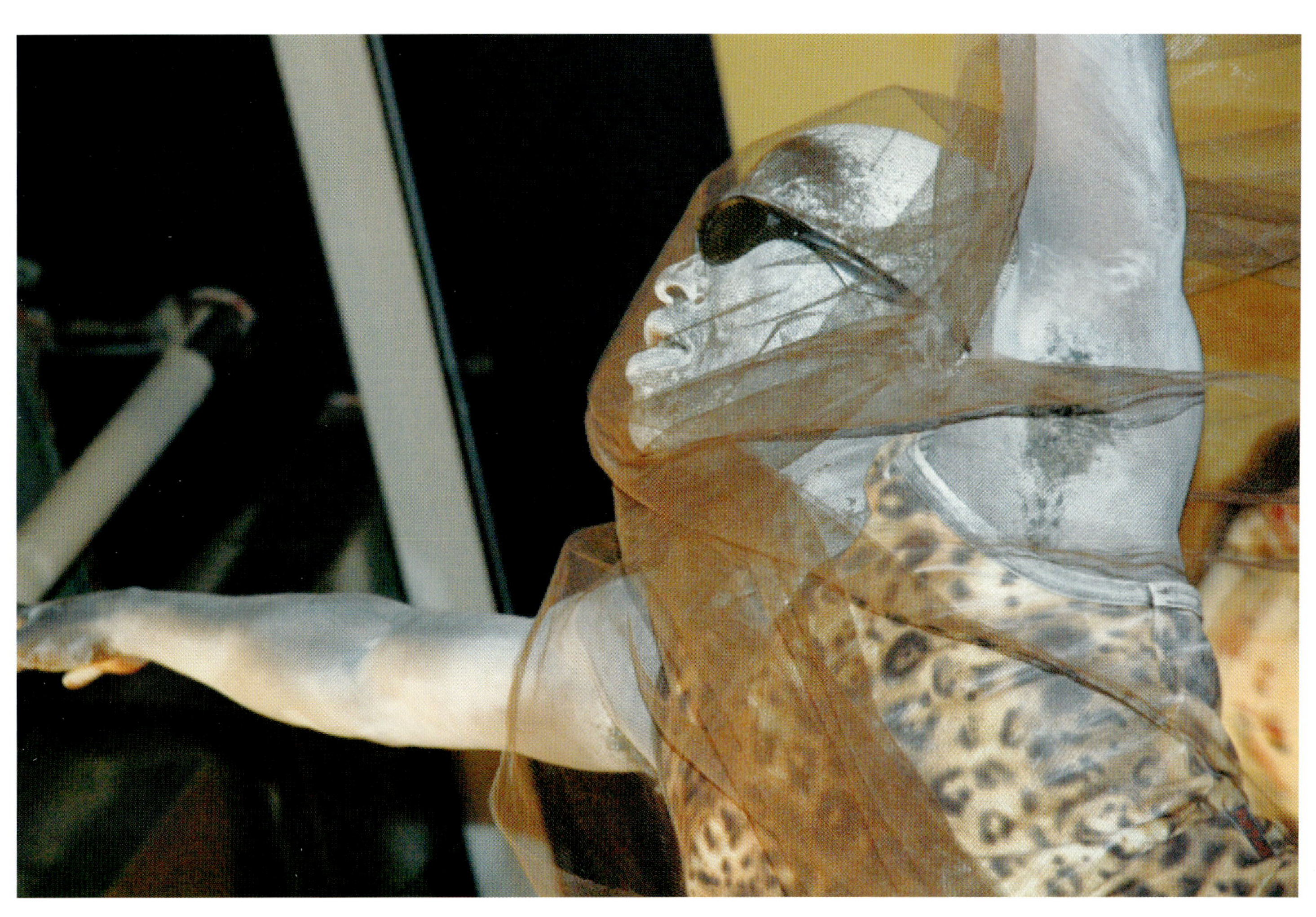

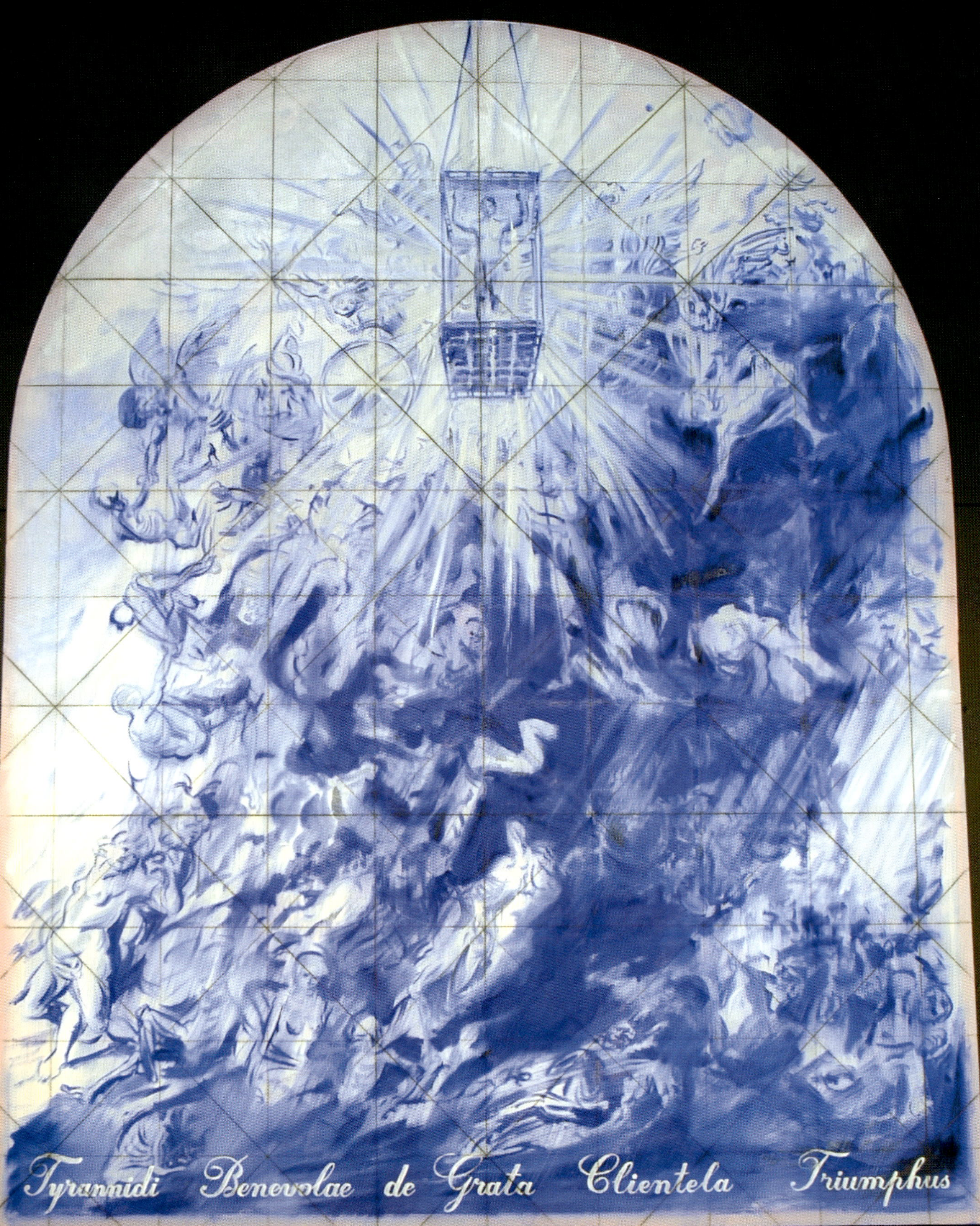
Tyrannidi Benevolae de Grata Clientela Triumphus

JOHANNES PHOKELA

Apotheosis
2004
Oil on canvas
270 X 214 CM
The Crossing, Cathedral of St John the Divine, 2004

Commissioned by *Season South Africa* for *Personal Affects*
Courtesy of the artist

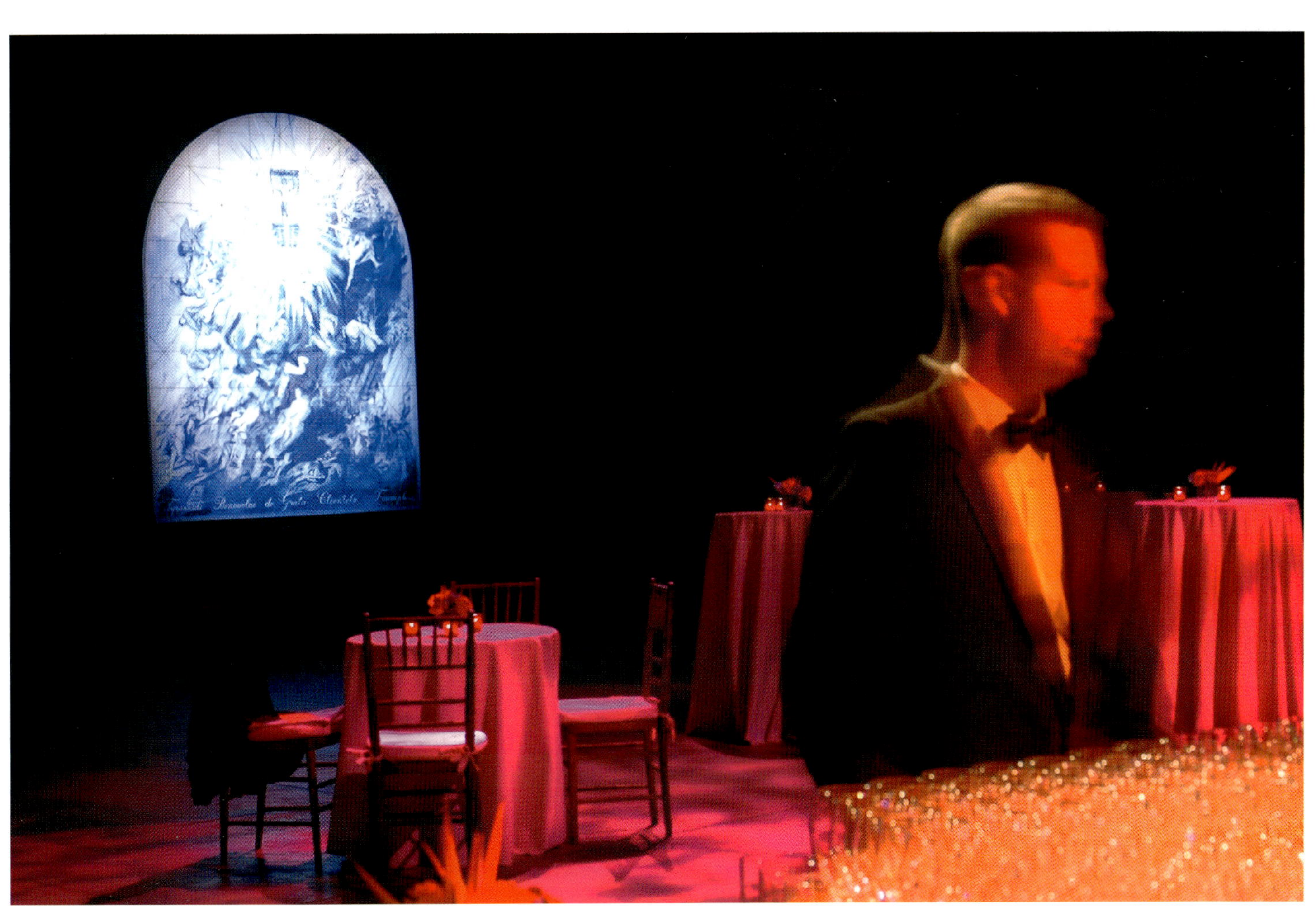

Fall of the Damned
1993
Diptych
Left-hand panel: Oil on canvas
Right-hand panel: Canvas, rabbit skin glue,
cotton twine, enamel paint
287.5 X 223.5 X 4 CM EACH
Museum for African Art, 2004

Courtesy of the artist

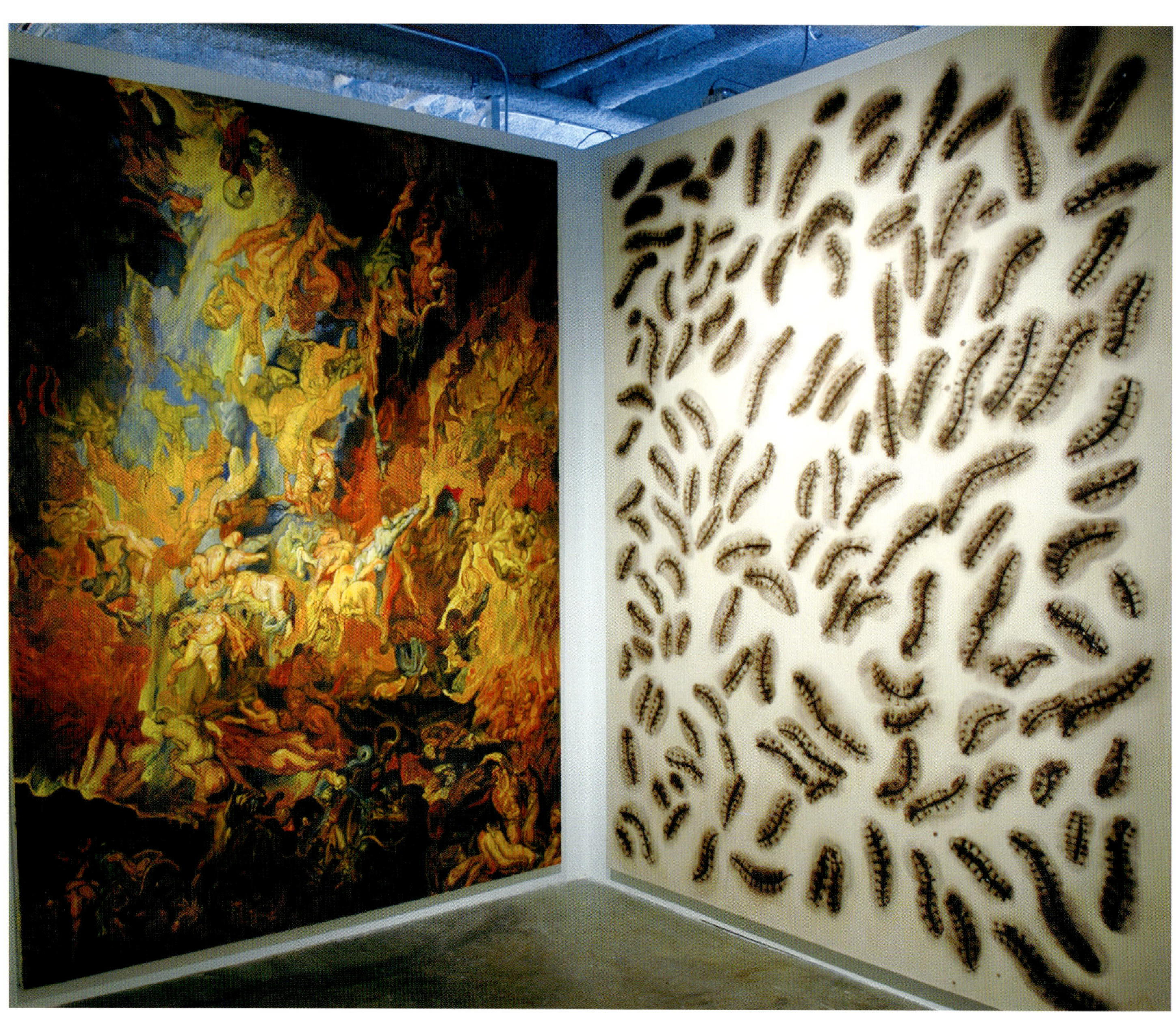

Diamonds and Bananas are Forever
1993
Acrylic paint on canvas, rabbit skin glue,
cotton twine, enamel paint
287.5 X 223.5 X 4 CM
Museum for African Art, 2004

Courtesy of the artist

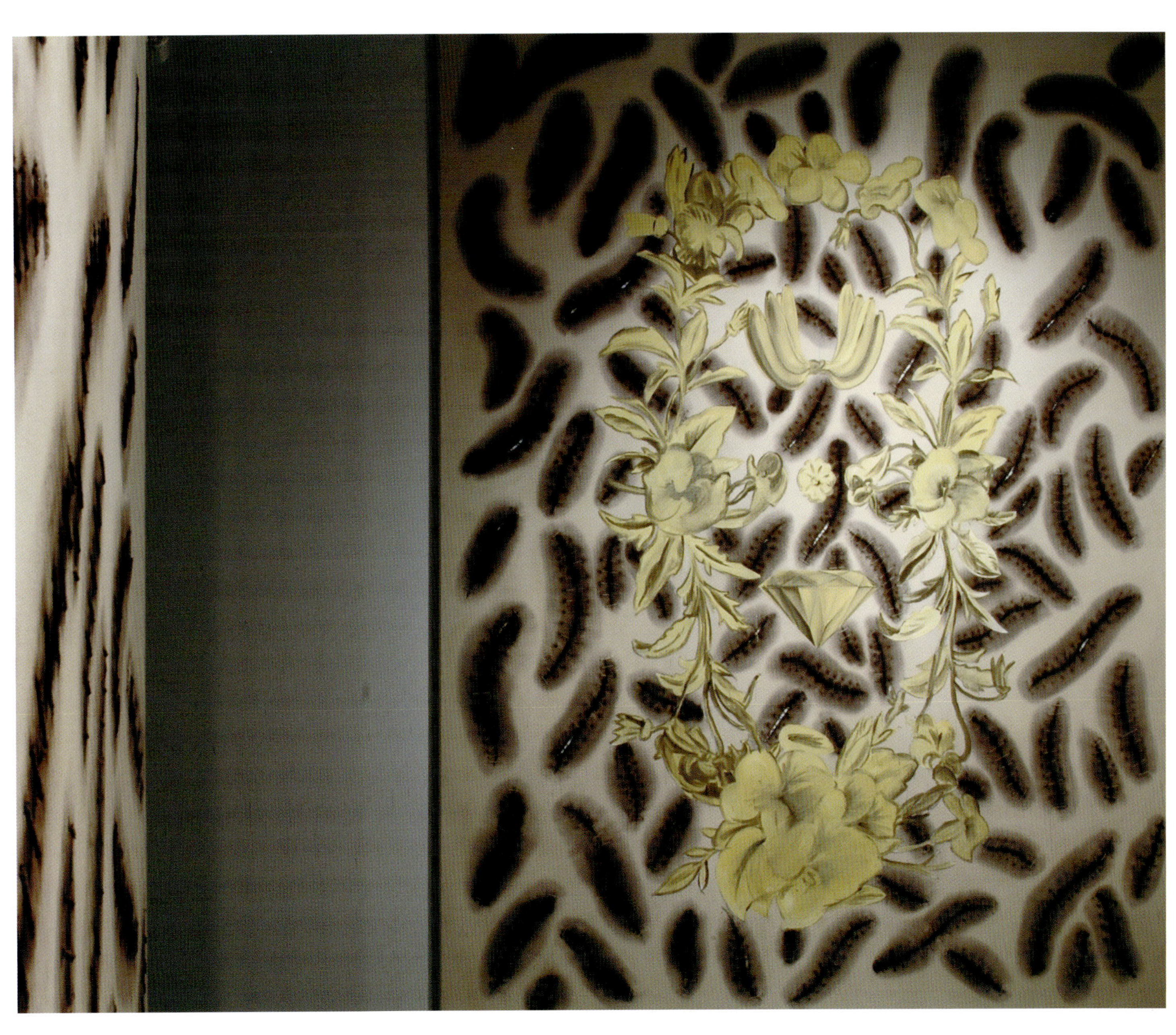

Vacuum Cleaner — Scooter.

R O B I N   R H O D E

Autonomous Drawing Project
2004
Slide projection
DIMENSIONS VARIABLE
Museum for African Art, 2004

Commissioned by *Season South Africa* for *Personal Affects*
Courtesy of the artist and Perry Rubenstein Gallery, New York

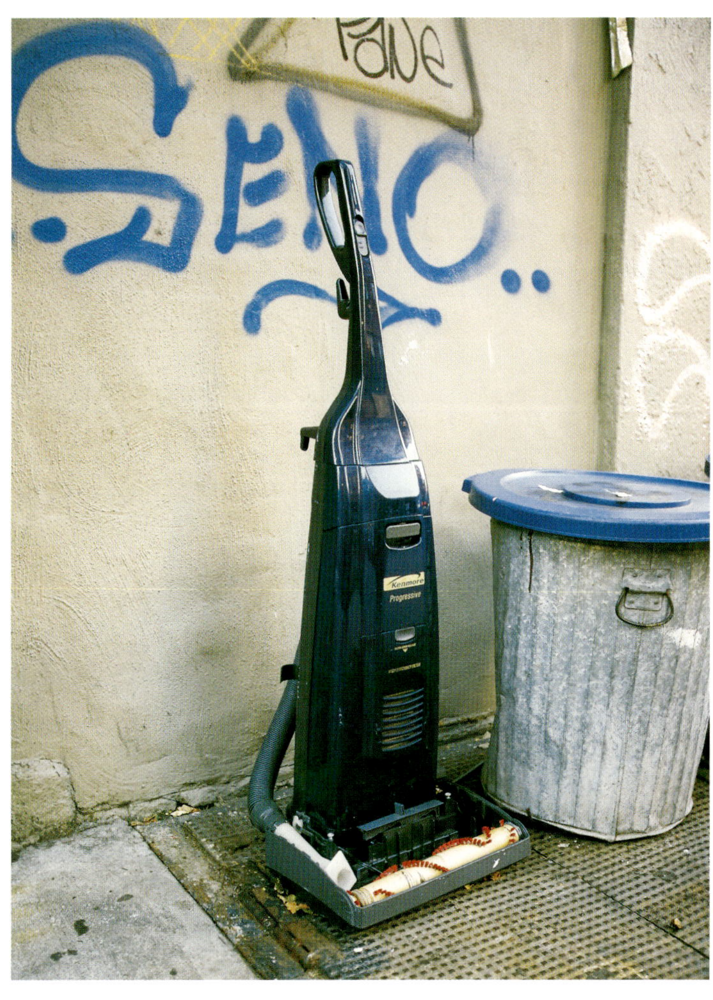

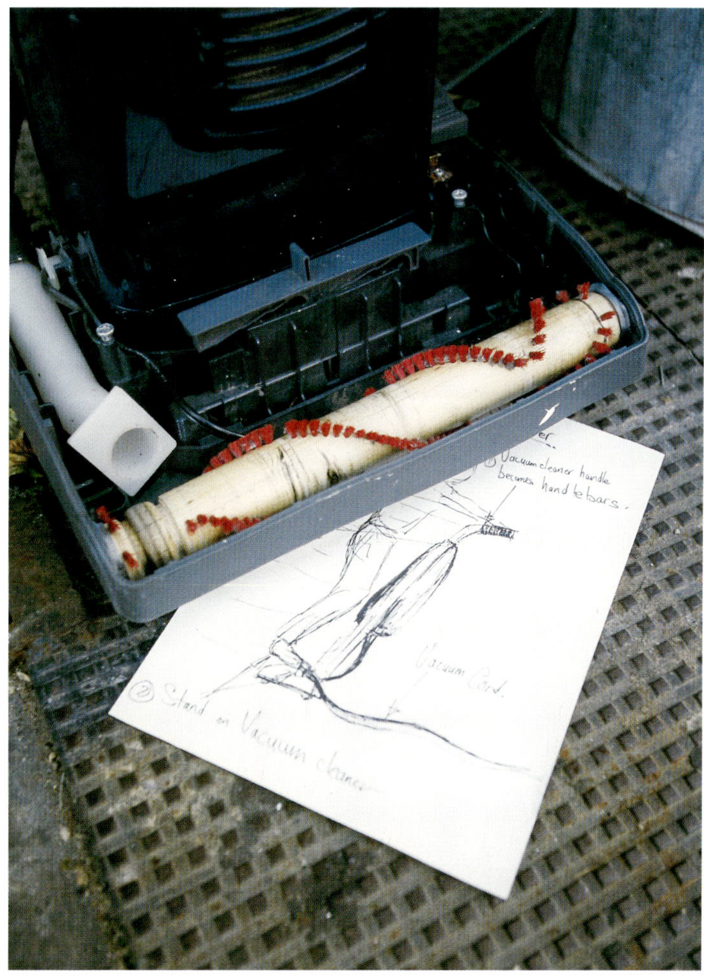

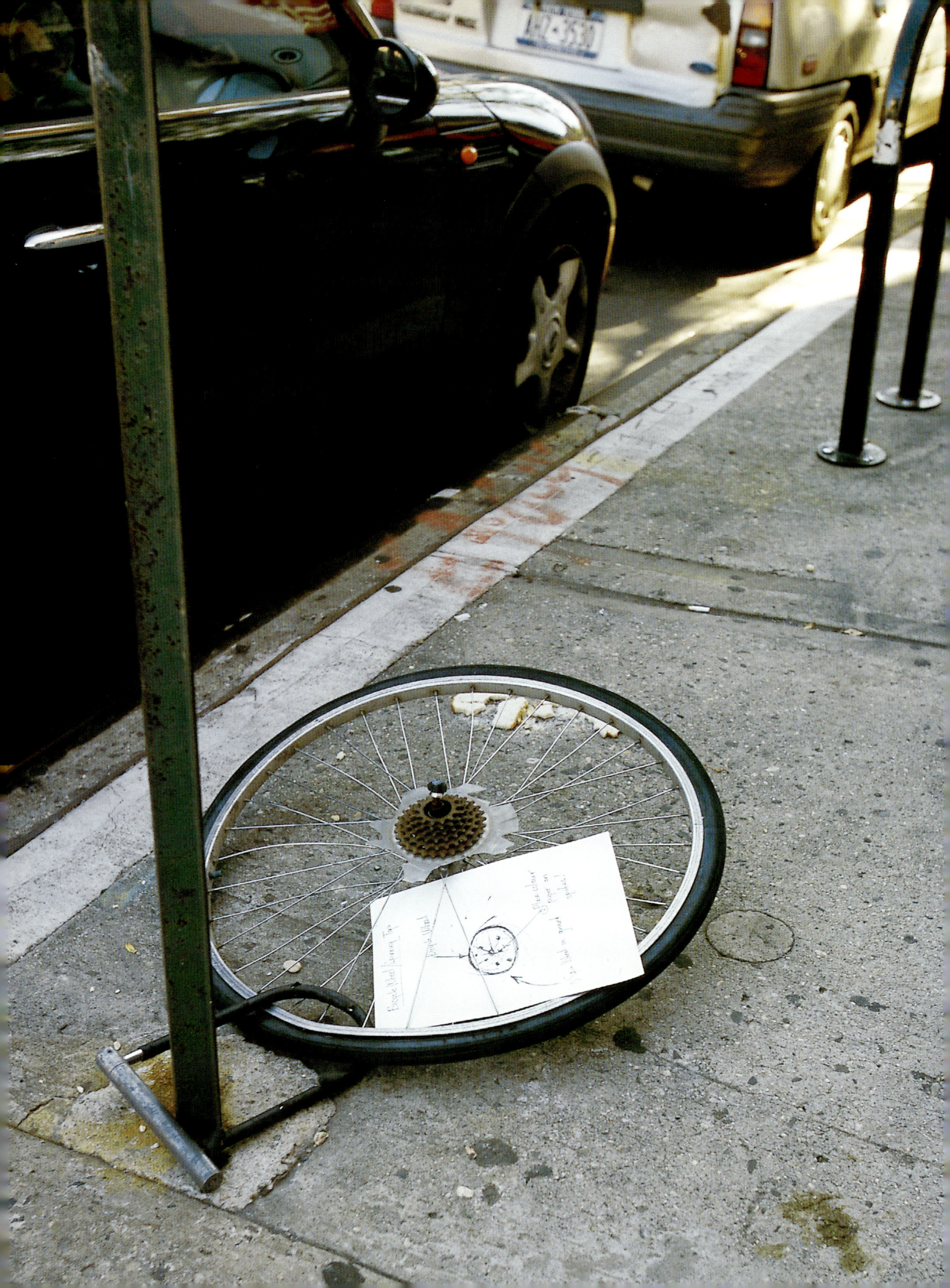

Bicycle Wheel Apering Top
Bicycle Wheel

Autonomous Drawing Project
2004
Slide projection
DIMENSIONS VARIABLE
Museum for African Art, 2004

Commissioned by *Season South Africa* for *Personal Affects*
Courtesy of the artist and Perry Rubenstein Gallery, New York

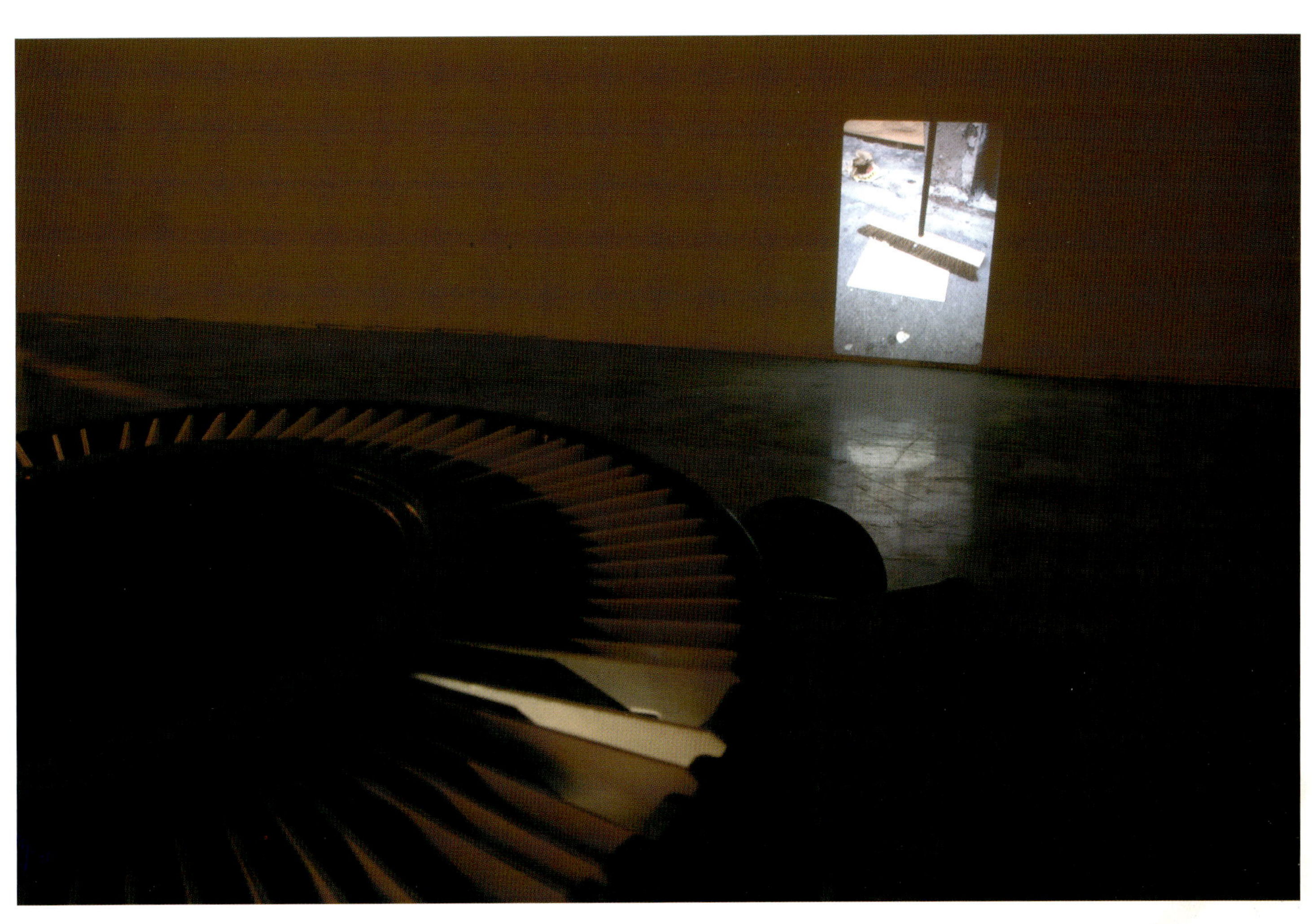

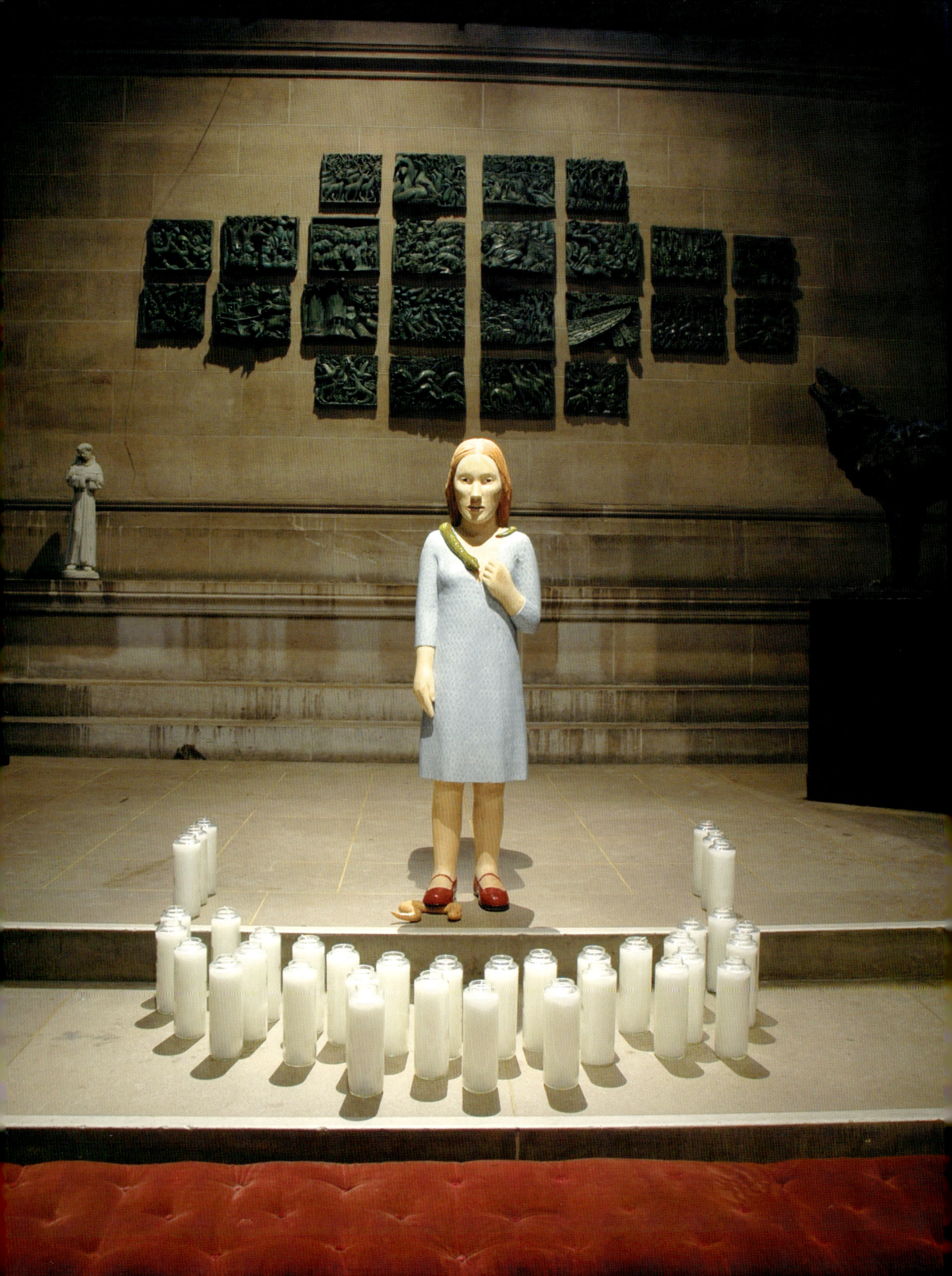

CLAUDETTE SCHREUDERS

The Free Girl
2004
Jacaranda wood, enamel paint
123 CM HIGH
Religious Life Bay, Cathedral of St John the Divine, 2004

Commissioned by *Season South Africa* for *Personal Affects*
Courtesy of the artist and Jack Shainman Gallery

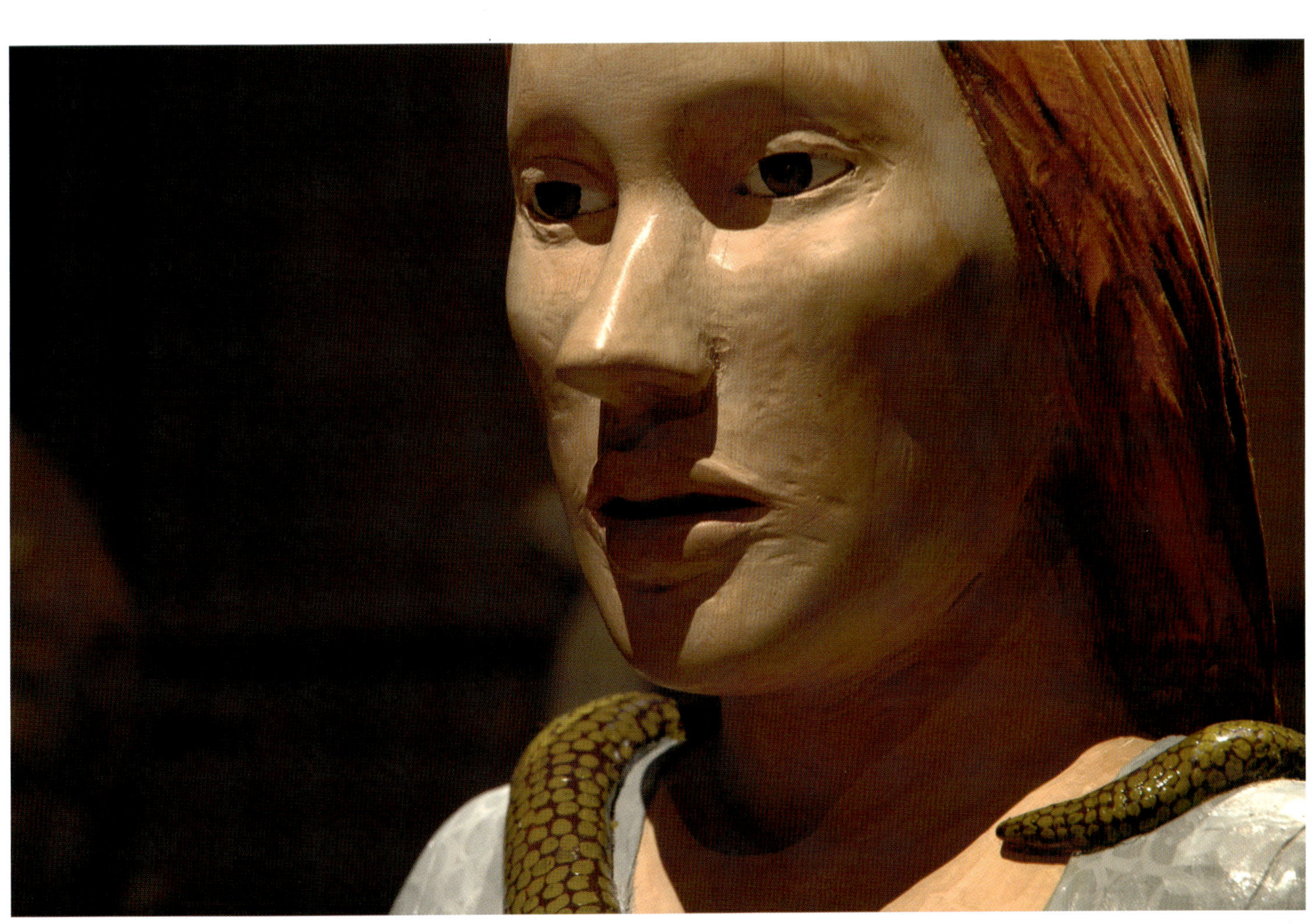

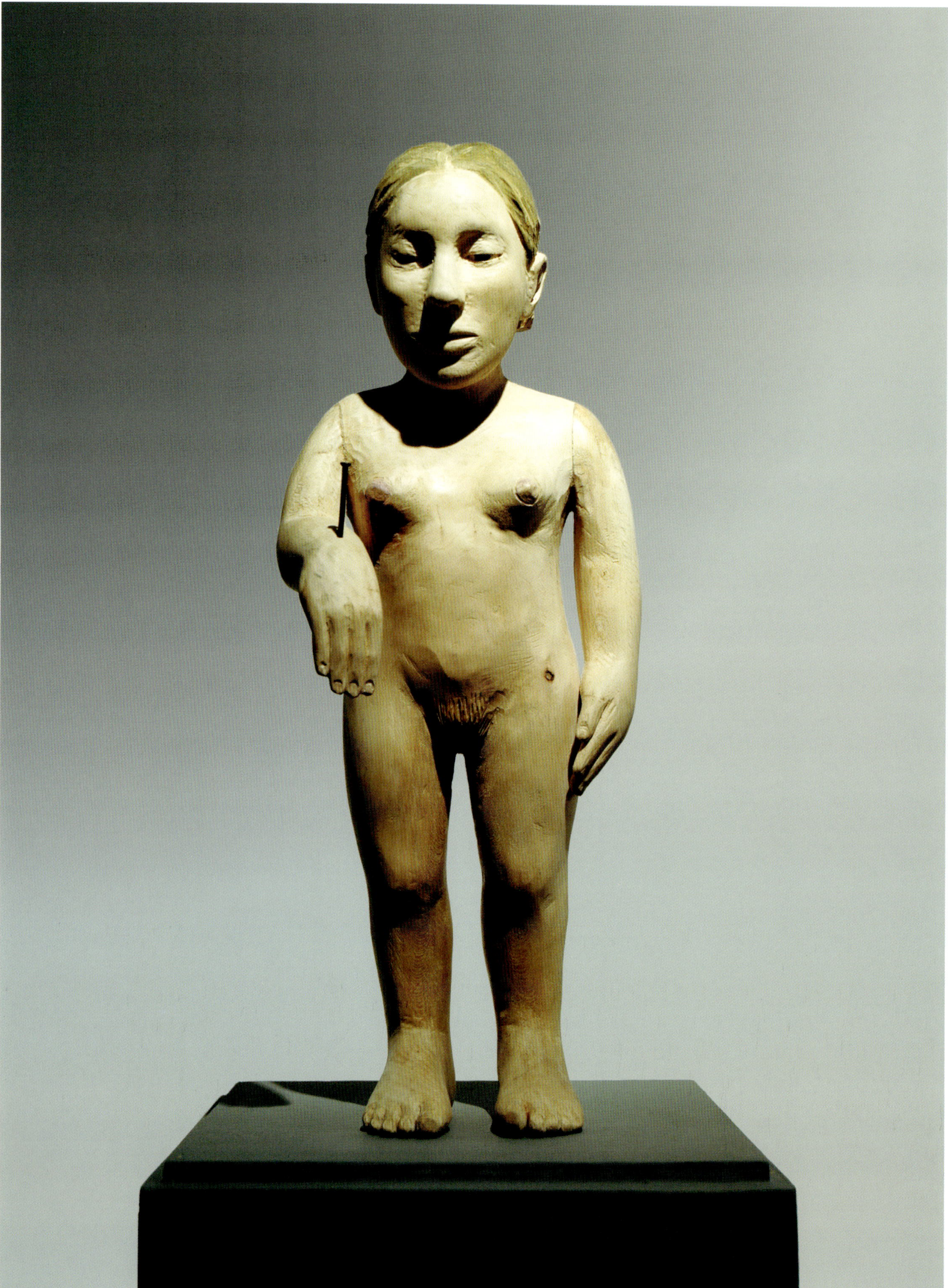

Fetish
2004
Plane wood, enamel paint
60 CM HIGH
Museum for African Art, 2004

Commissioned by *Season South Africa* for *Personal Affects*
Courtesy of the artist and Jack Shainman Gallery

Untitled
2004
Pencil drawings
102 X 64 CM EACH
Museum for African Art, 2004

Commissioned by *Season South Africa* for *Personal Affects*
Courtesy of the artist and Jack Shainman Gallery

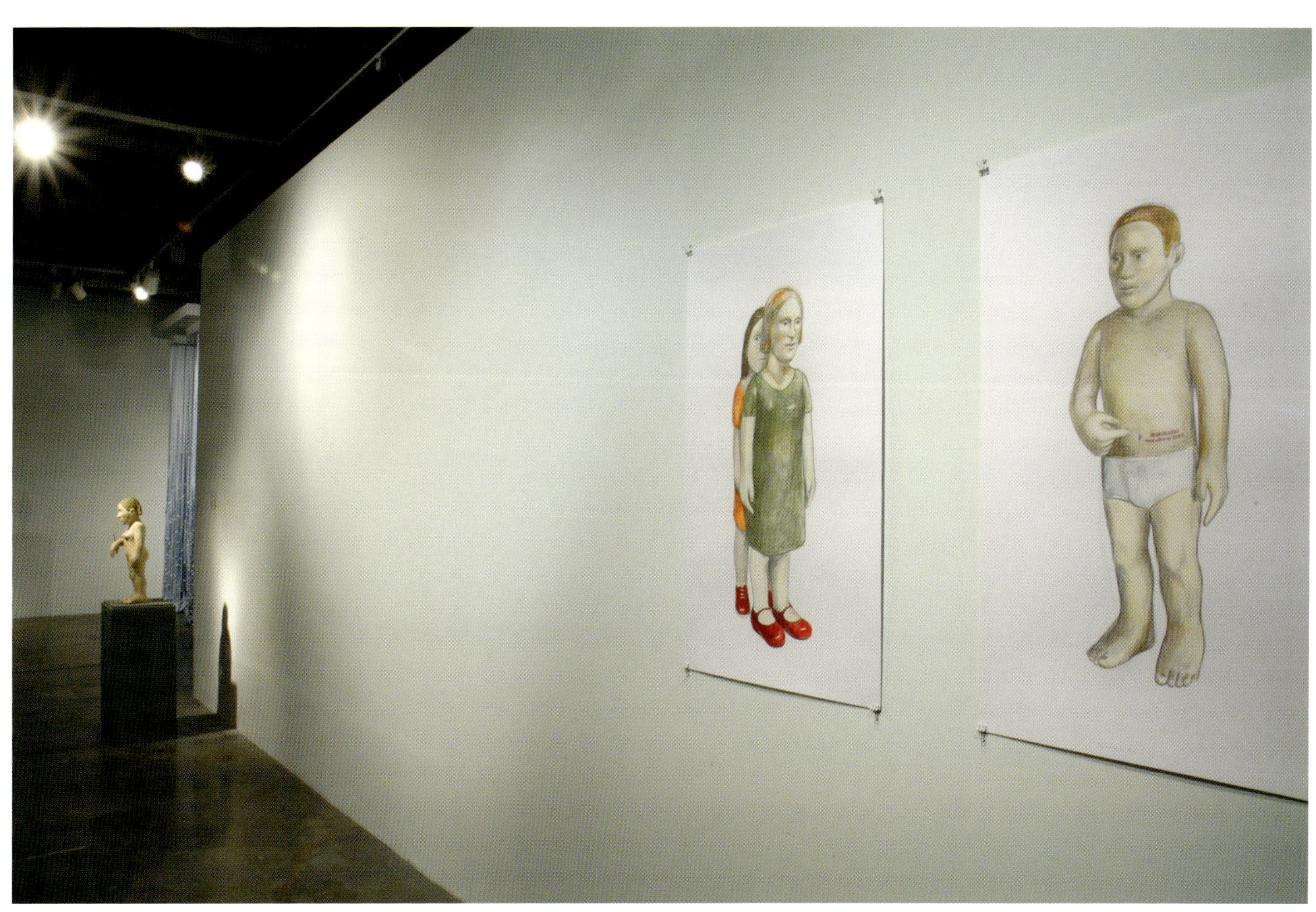

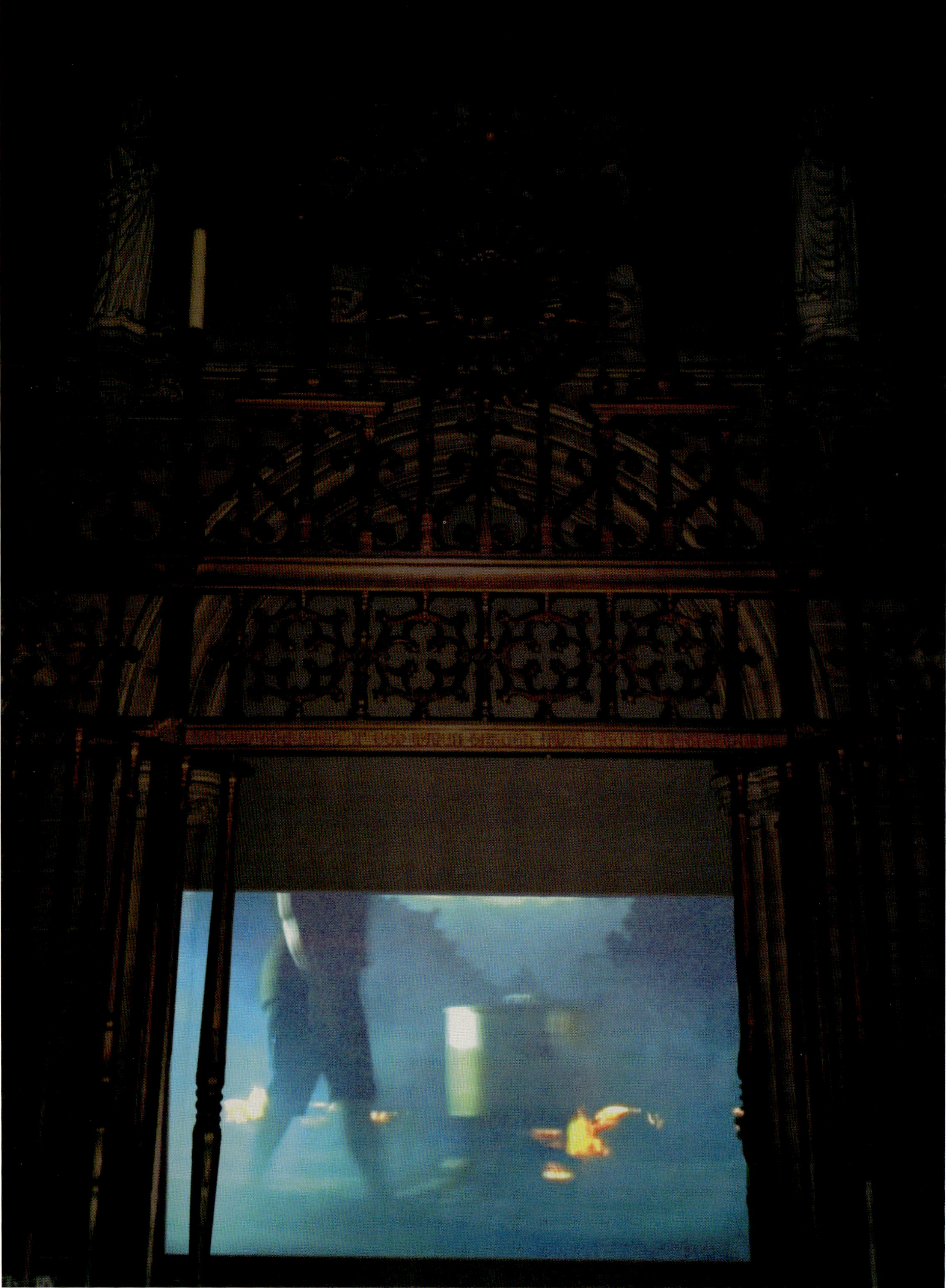

BERNI SEARLE

Vapour
2004
DVD projection, shot on S16mm film
DURATION 4 MIN 9 SEC
Entrance to the Baptistry, Cathedral of St John the Divine, 2004

Courtesy of the artist and Michael Stevenson Contemporary
Produced, for *Personal Affects*, with the assistance of *Season South Africa*

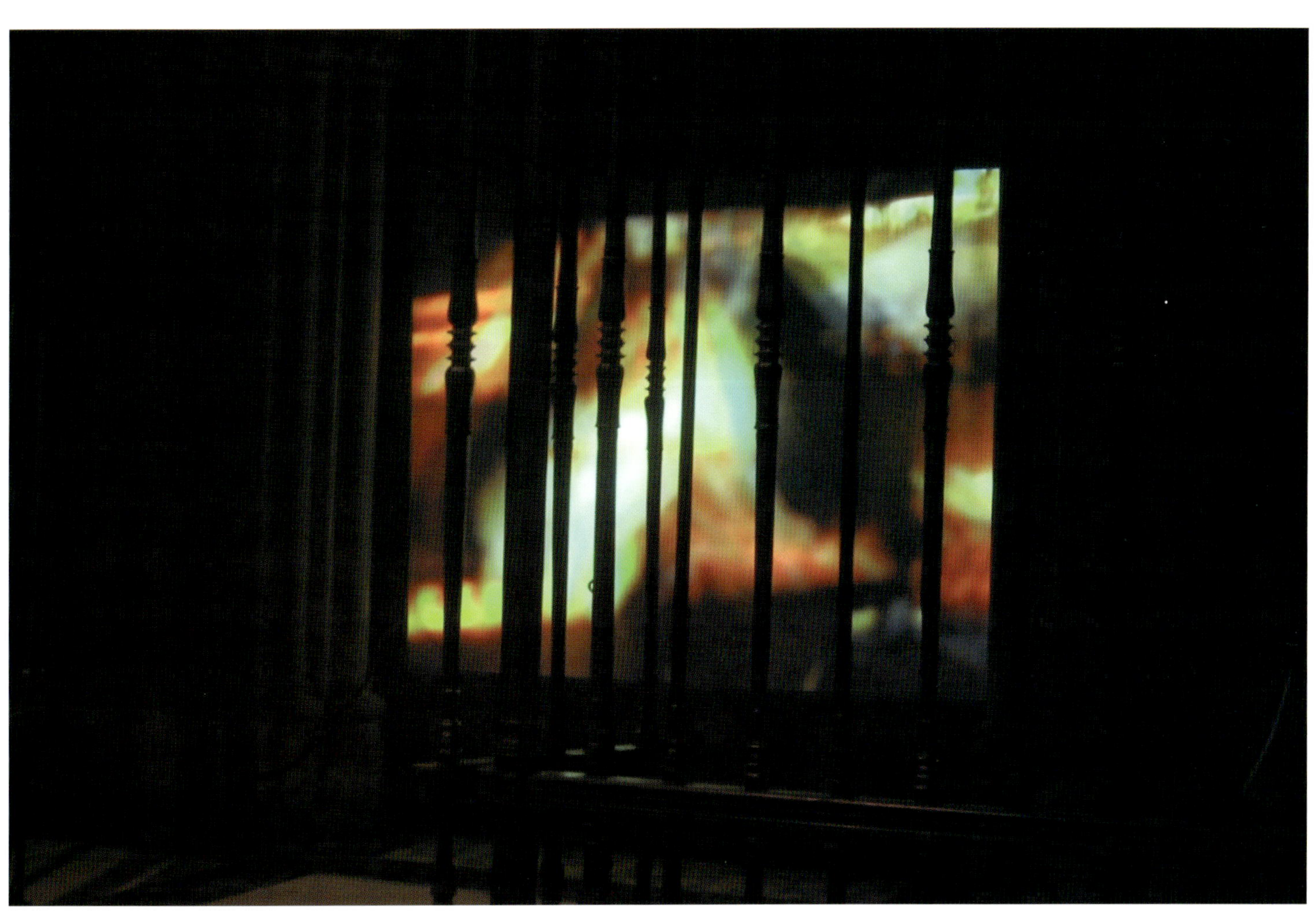

In Light Of I – IV
2004
Hand-printed colour photographs
100 X 121 CM EACH
Museum for African Art, 2004

Courtesy of the artist and Michael Stevenson Contemporary

Half Light
2004
Lambda print
173 x 360CM
Museum for African Art, 2004

Courtesy of the artist and Michael Stevenson Contemporary

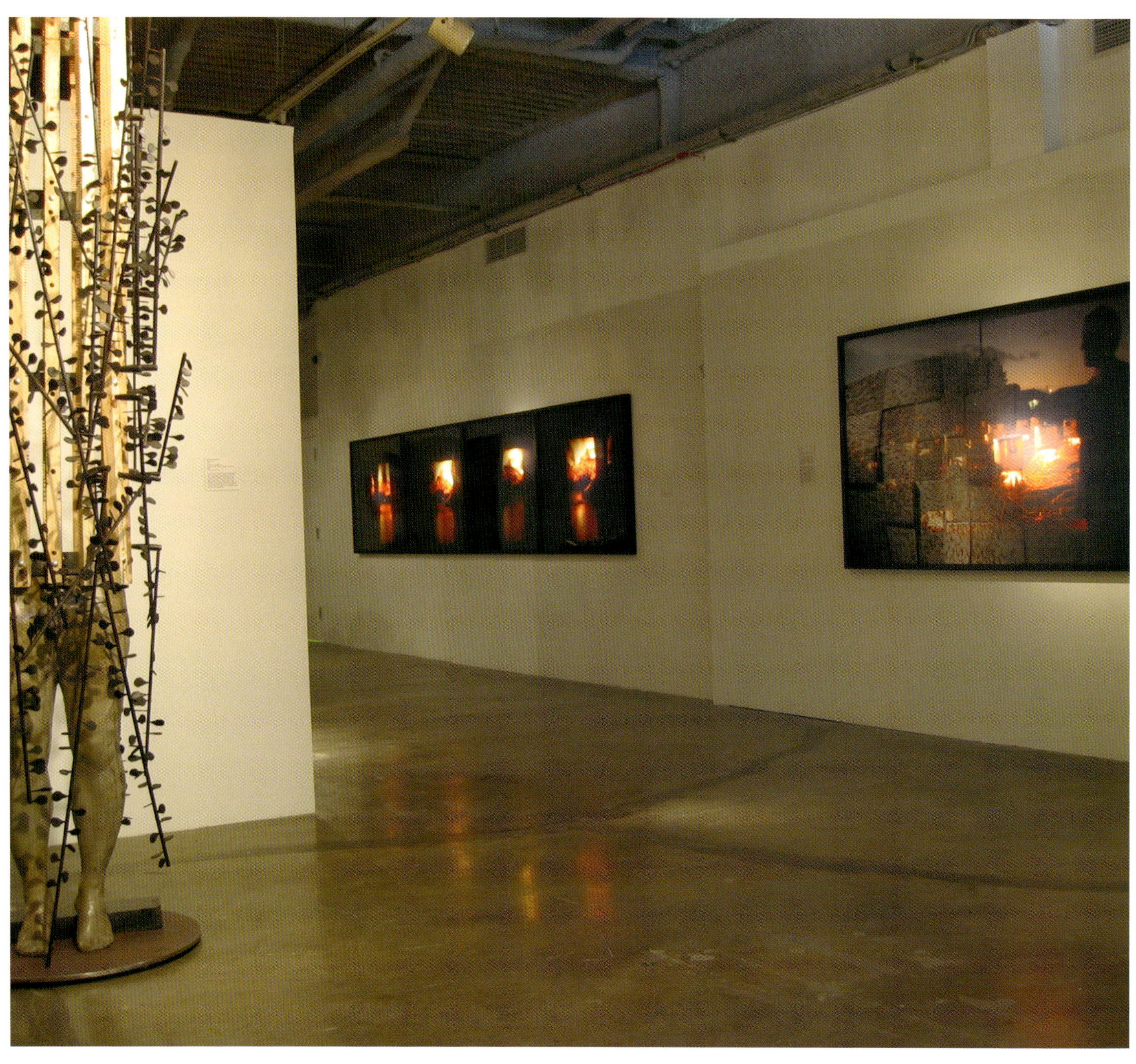

In Light Of I – IV
2004
Hand-printed colour photographs
100 X 121 CM EACH
Museum for African Art, 2004

Courtesy of the artist and Michael Stevenson Contemporary

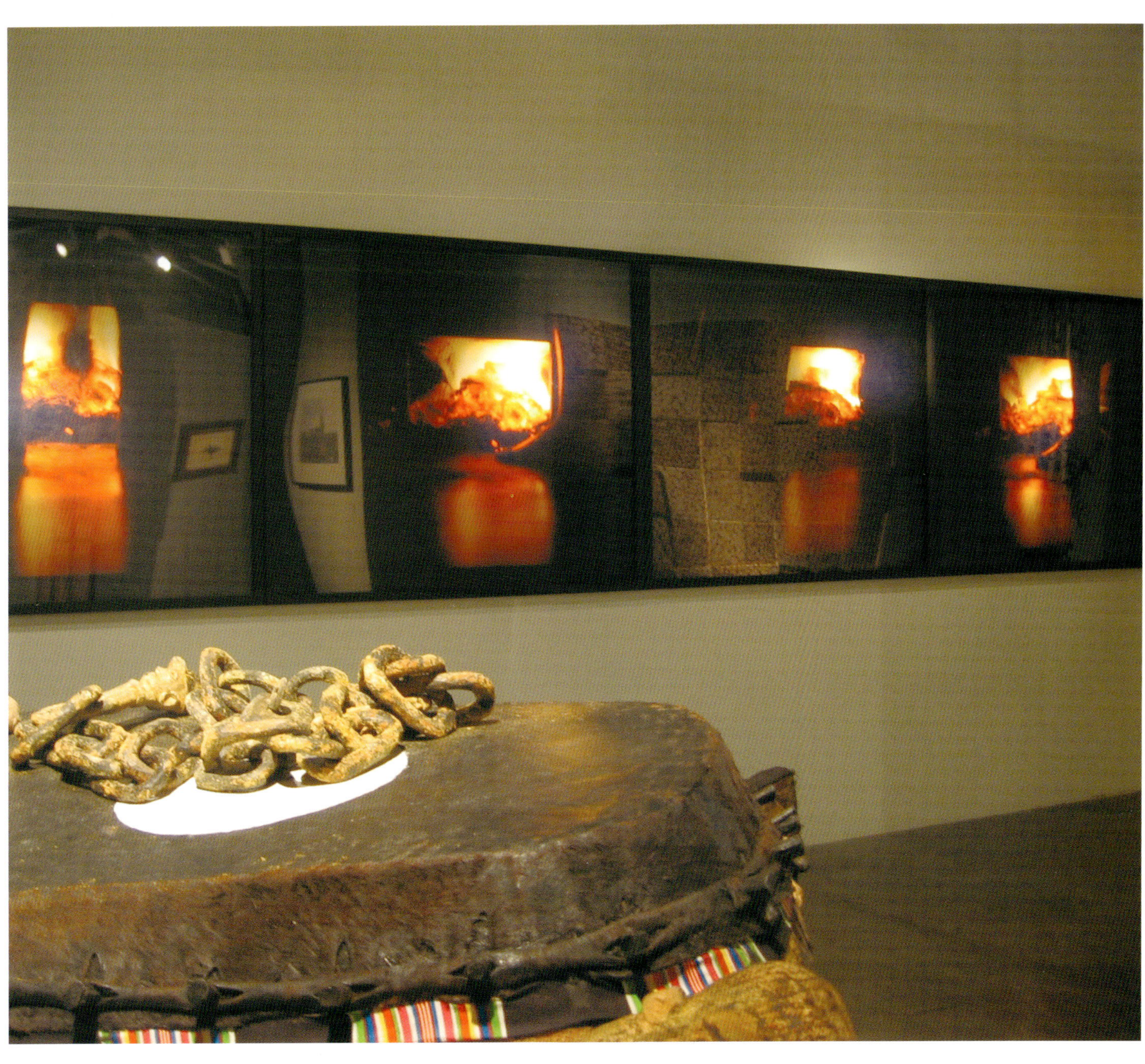

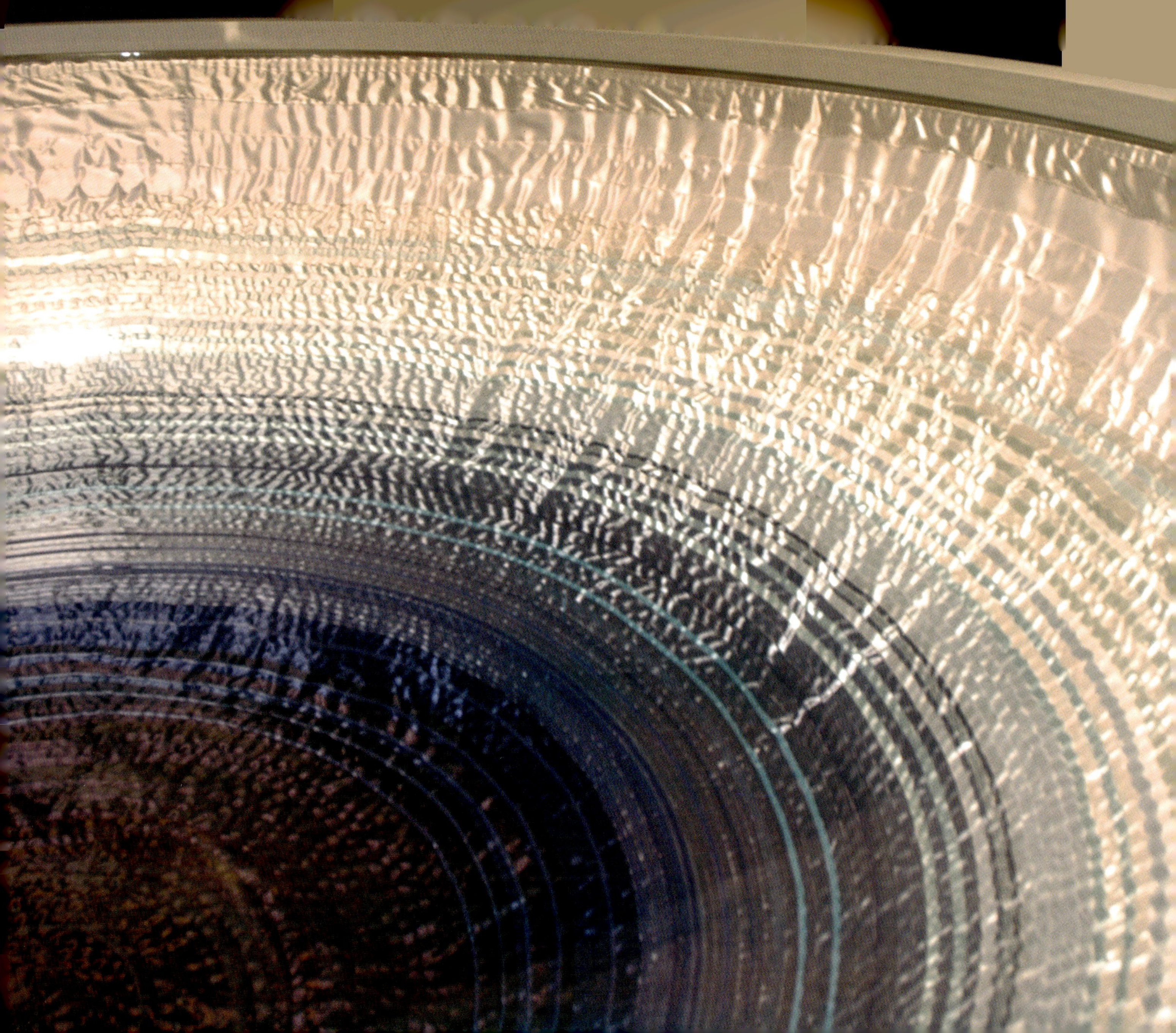

DOREEN SOUTHWOOD

Black Hole
2003
Satin ribbon, wood and perspex
180 CM DIAMETER
Education Bay, Cathedral of St John the Divine, 2004

Courtesy of the artist

The Swimmer
2004
Painted bronze
43 x 1150 x 200 CM
Education Bay, Cathedral of St John the Divine, 2004

Courtesy of the artist

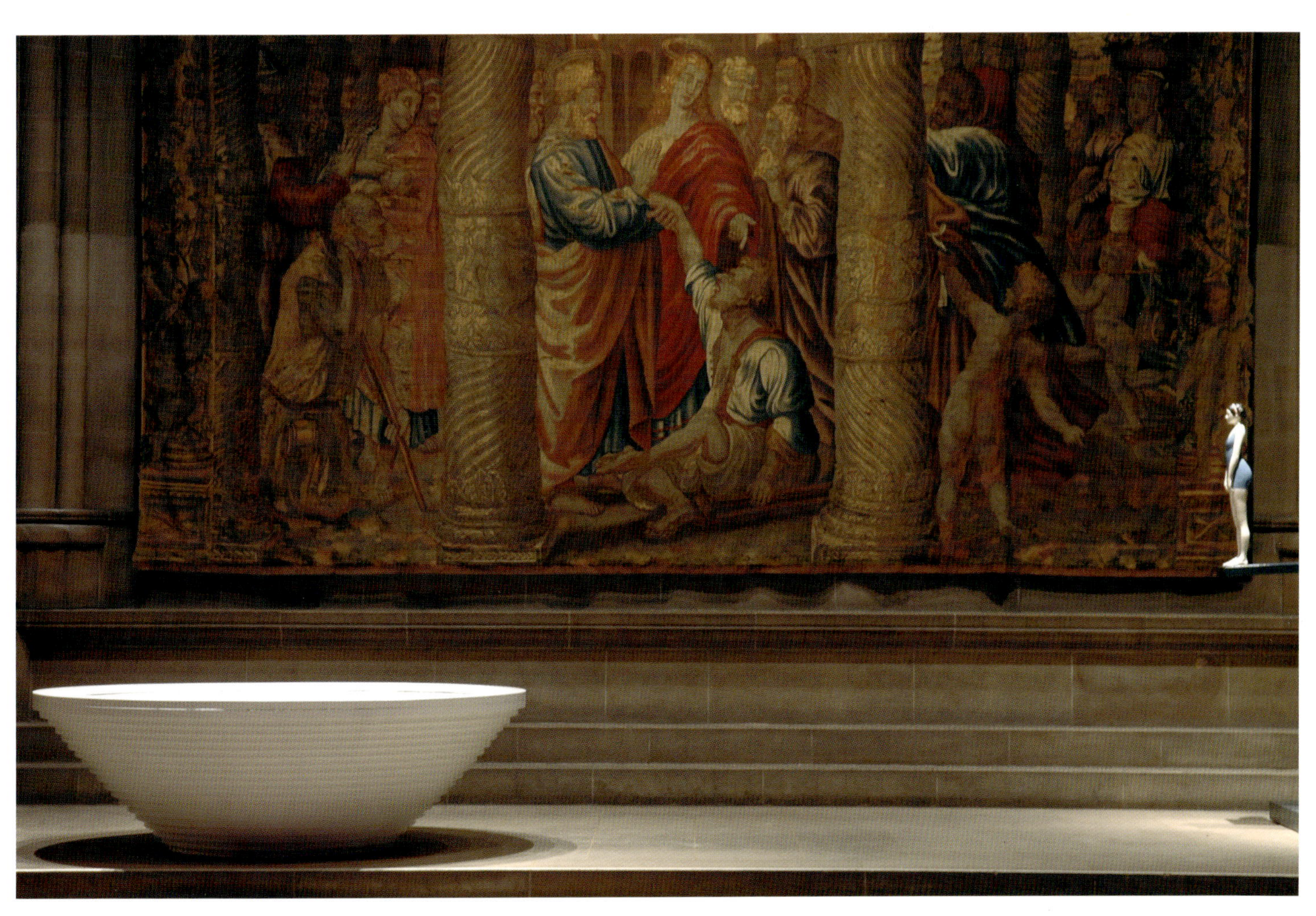

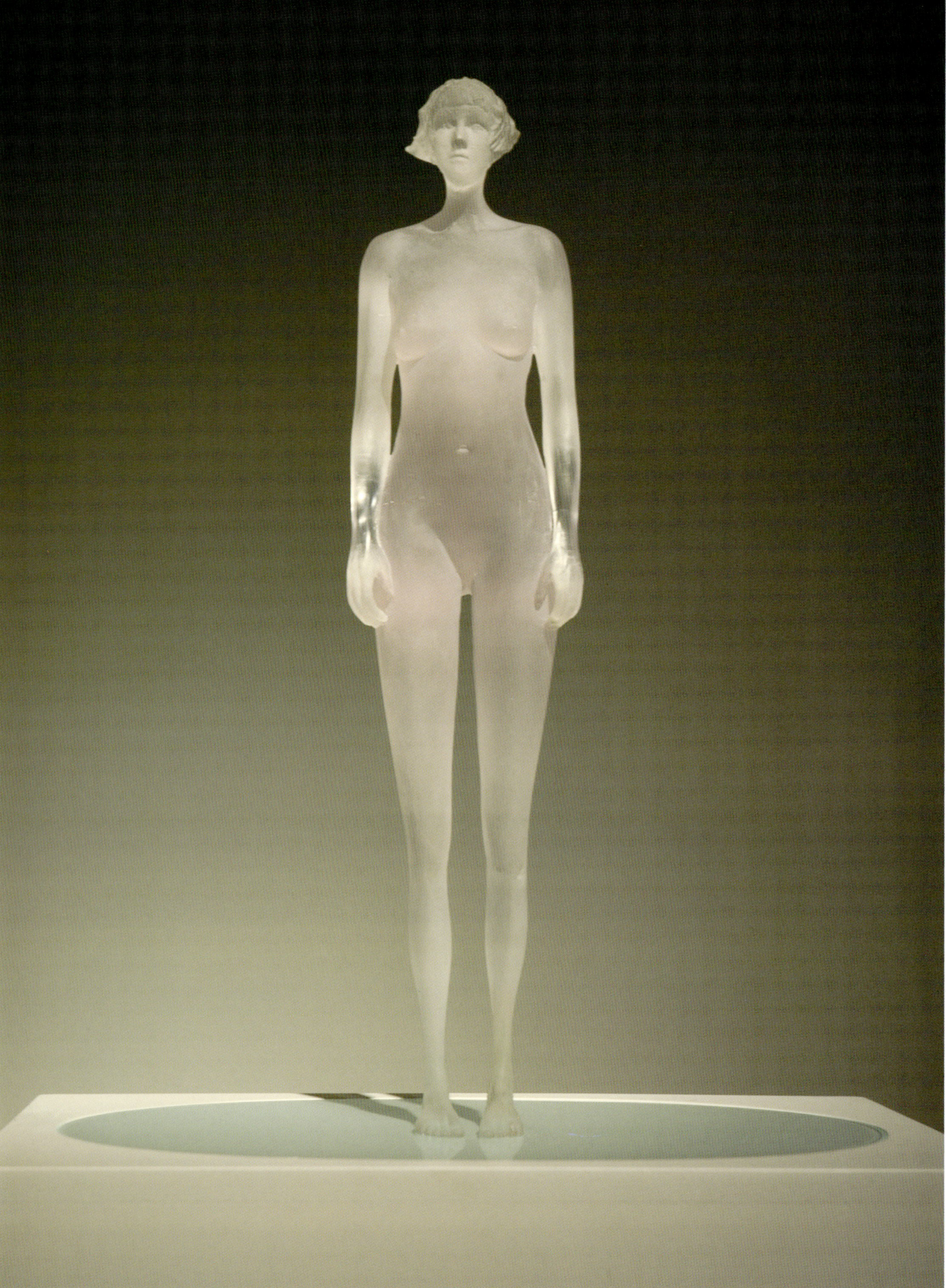

Untitled
2004
Casting resin
50 X 15 X 15 CM
Museum for African Art, 2004

Commissioned by *Season South Africa* for *Personal Affects*
Courtesy of the artist

Ribbon Pillars
2004
Satin ribbon and wood
400 CM HIGH
Museum for African Art, 2004

Commissioned by *Season South Africa* for *Personal Affects*
Courtesy of the artist

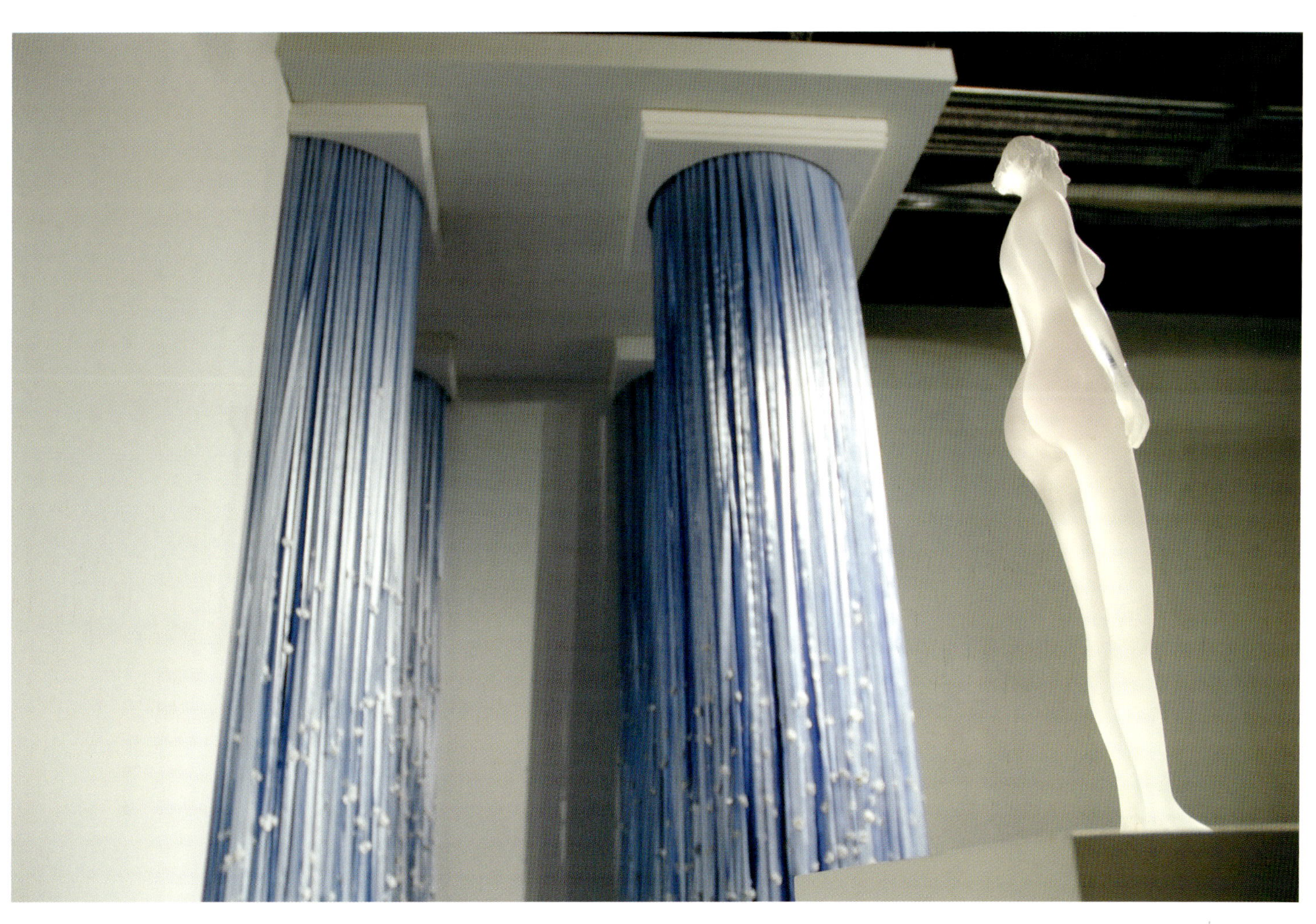

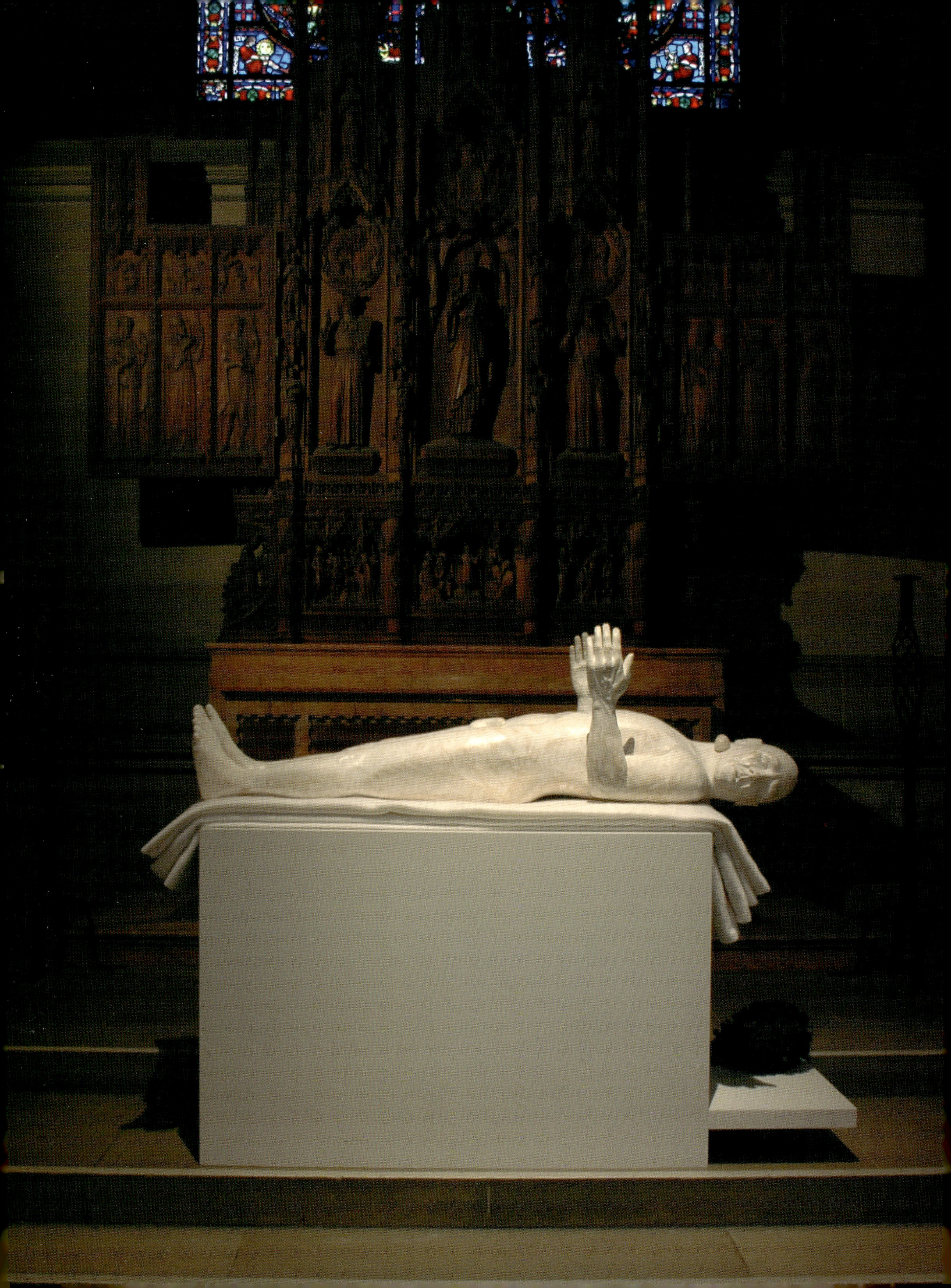

CLIVE VAN DEN BERG

Love's Ballast
2004
Wood, blankets
Lawyers Bay, Cathedral of St John the Divine, 2004

Commissioned by *Season South Africa* for *Personal Affects*
Courtesy of the artist

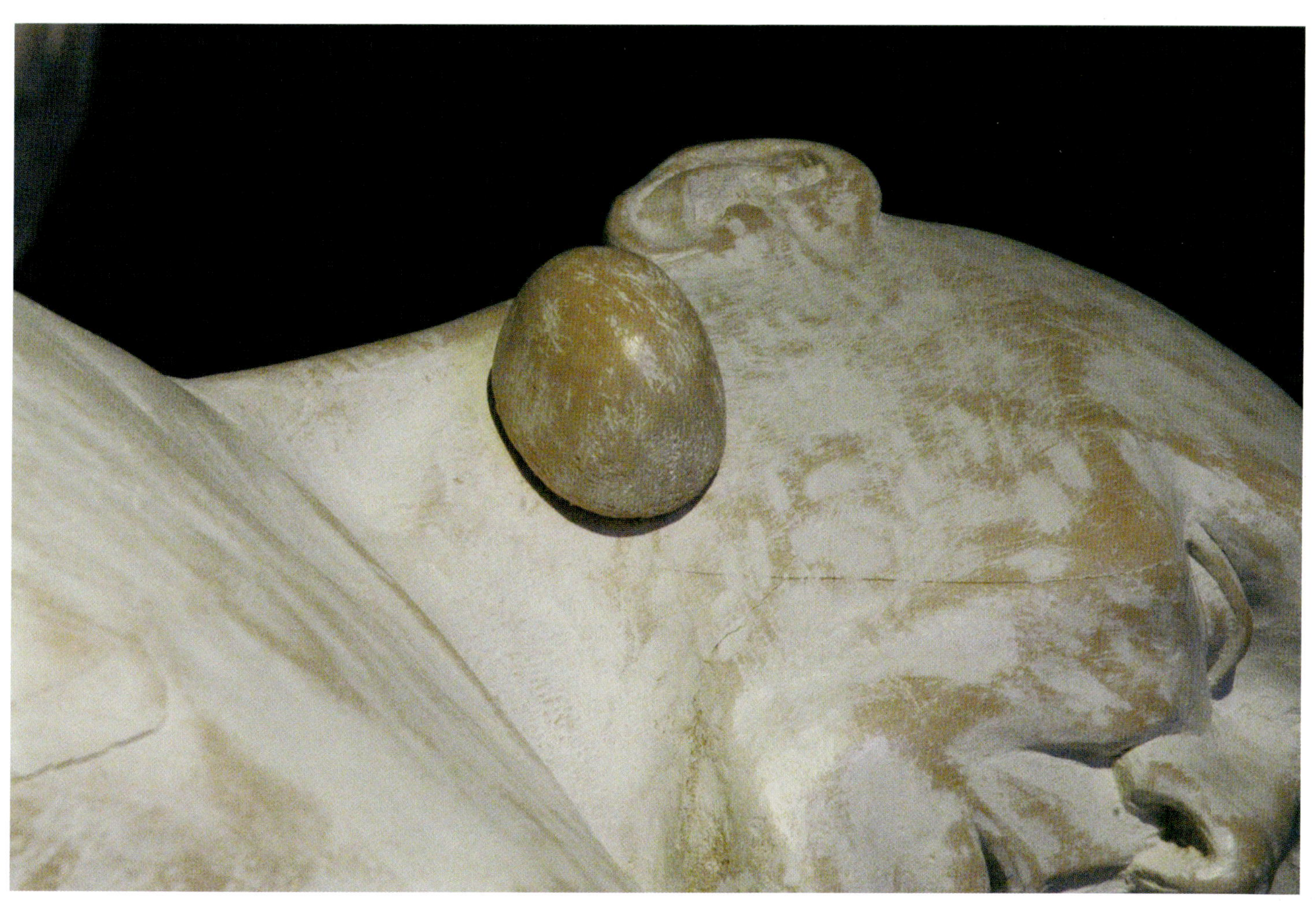

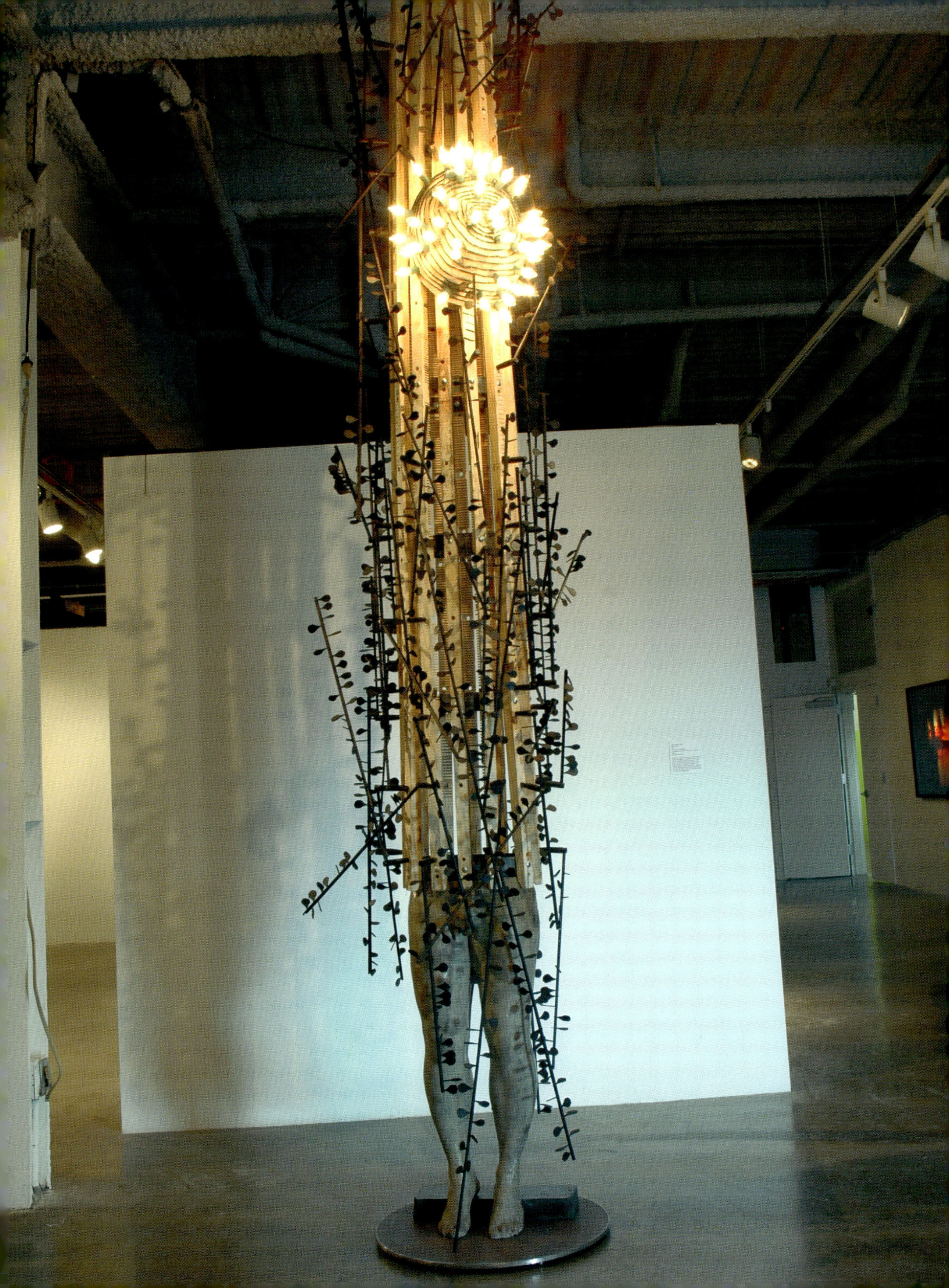

Family Tree II
2004
Cement, wood, lightbulbs
400 CM HIGH
Museum for African Art, 2004

Commissioned by *Season South Africa* for *Personal Affects*
Courtesy of the artist

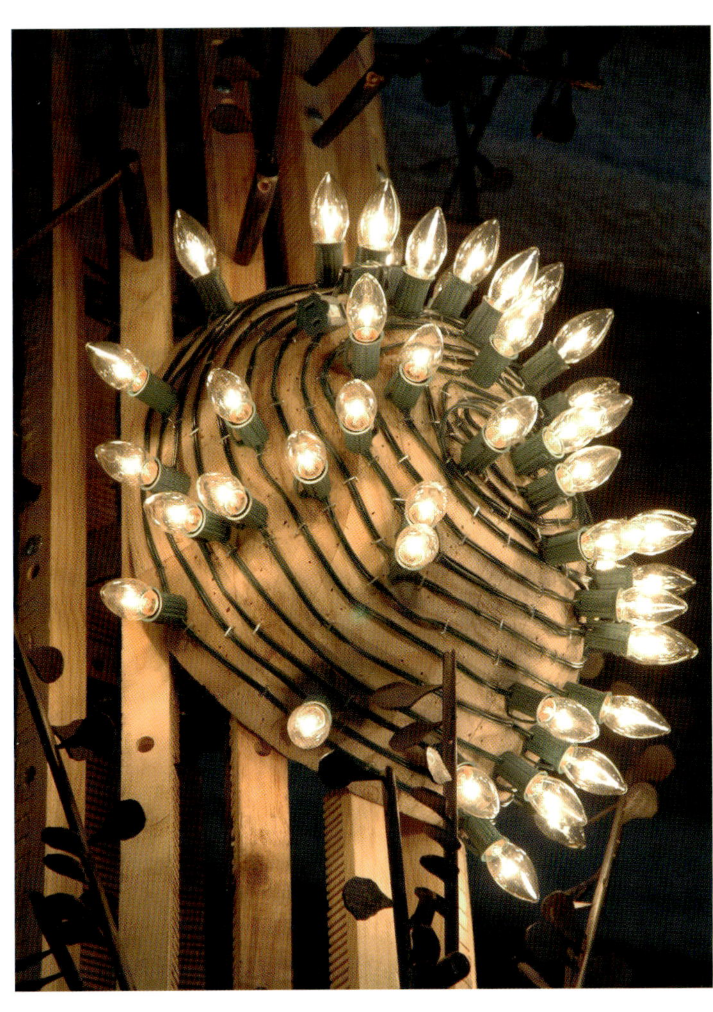
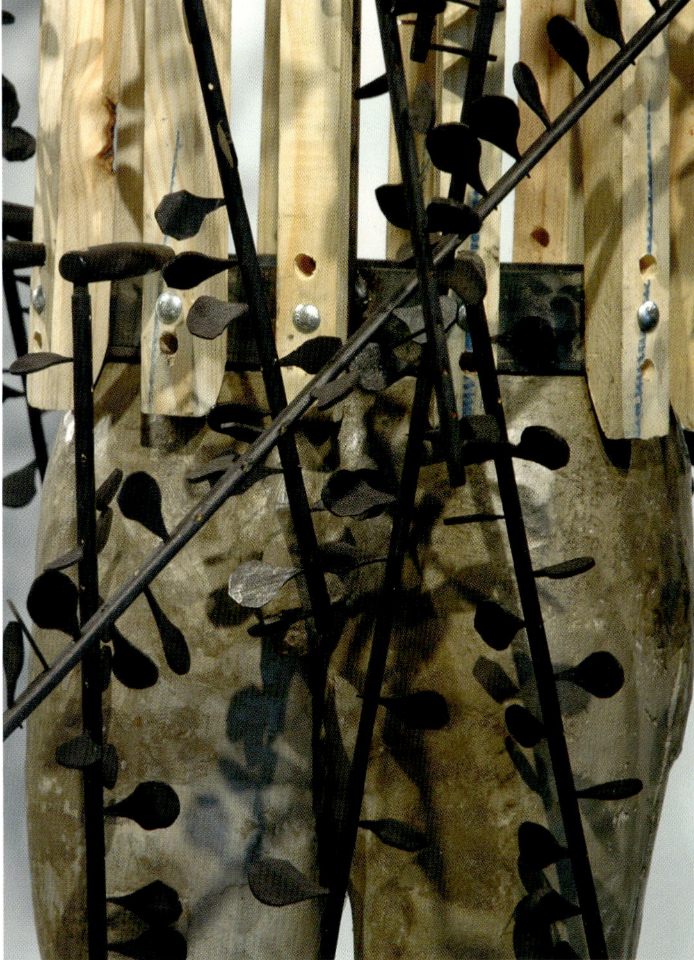

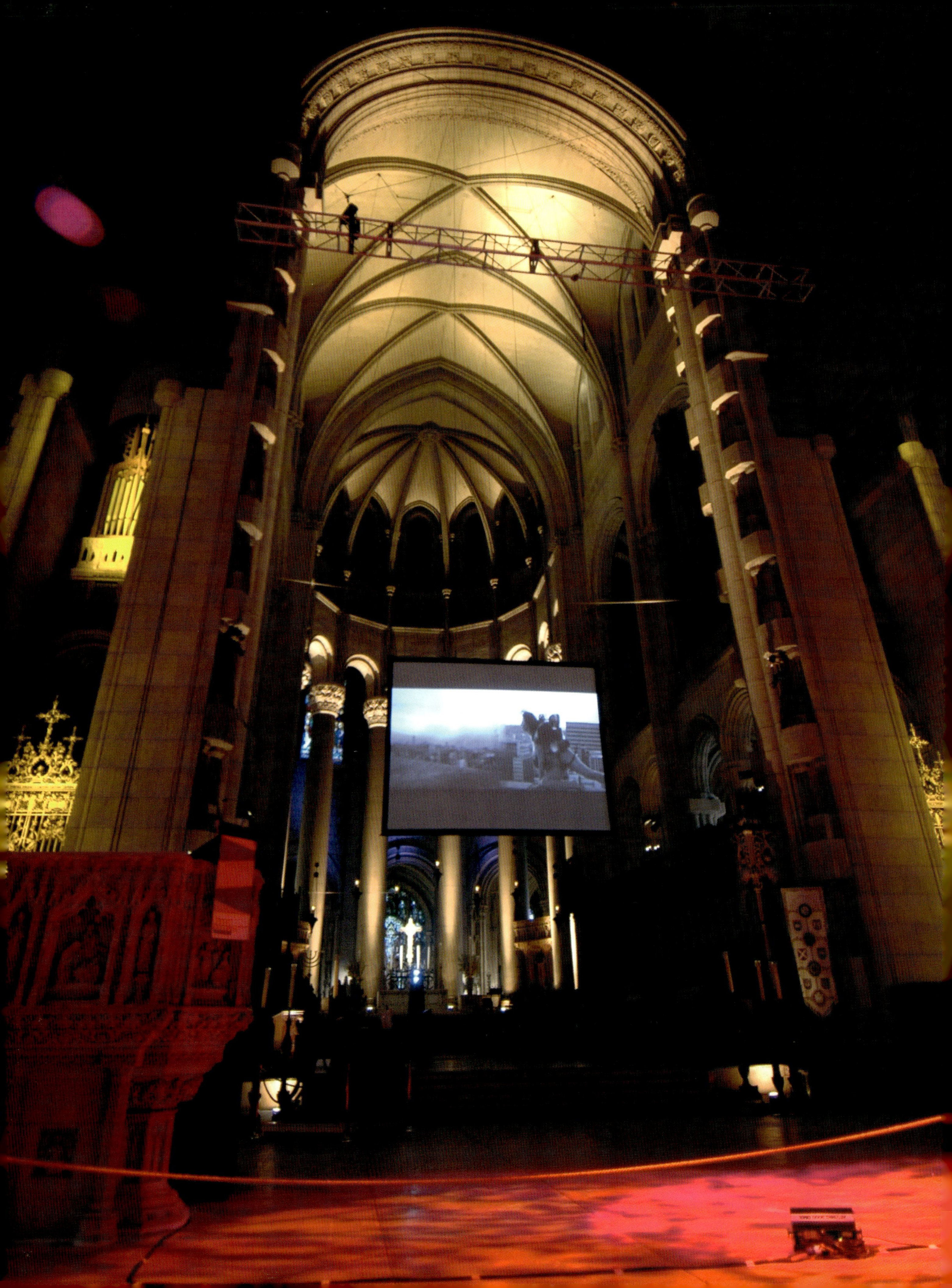

MINNETTE VÁRI

facing page
The Calling
2003
Video and audio installation
DURATION 3 MIN
The Crossing, Cathedral of St John the Divine, 23 September 2004

Courtesy of the artist and Serge Ziegler Gallery

this page
The Calling
2003
Video and audio installation
DURATION 3 MIN
Chapel of St Columba, Cathedral of St John the Divine, 2004

Courtesy of the artist and Serge Ziegler Gallery

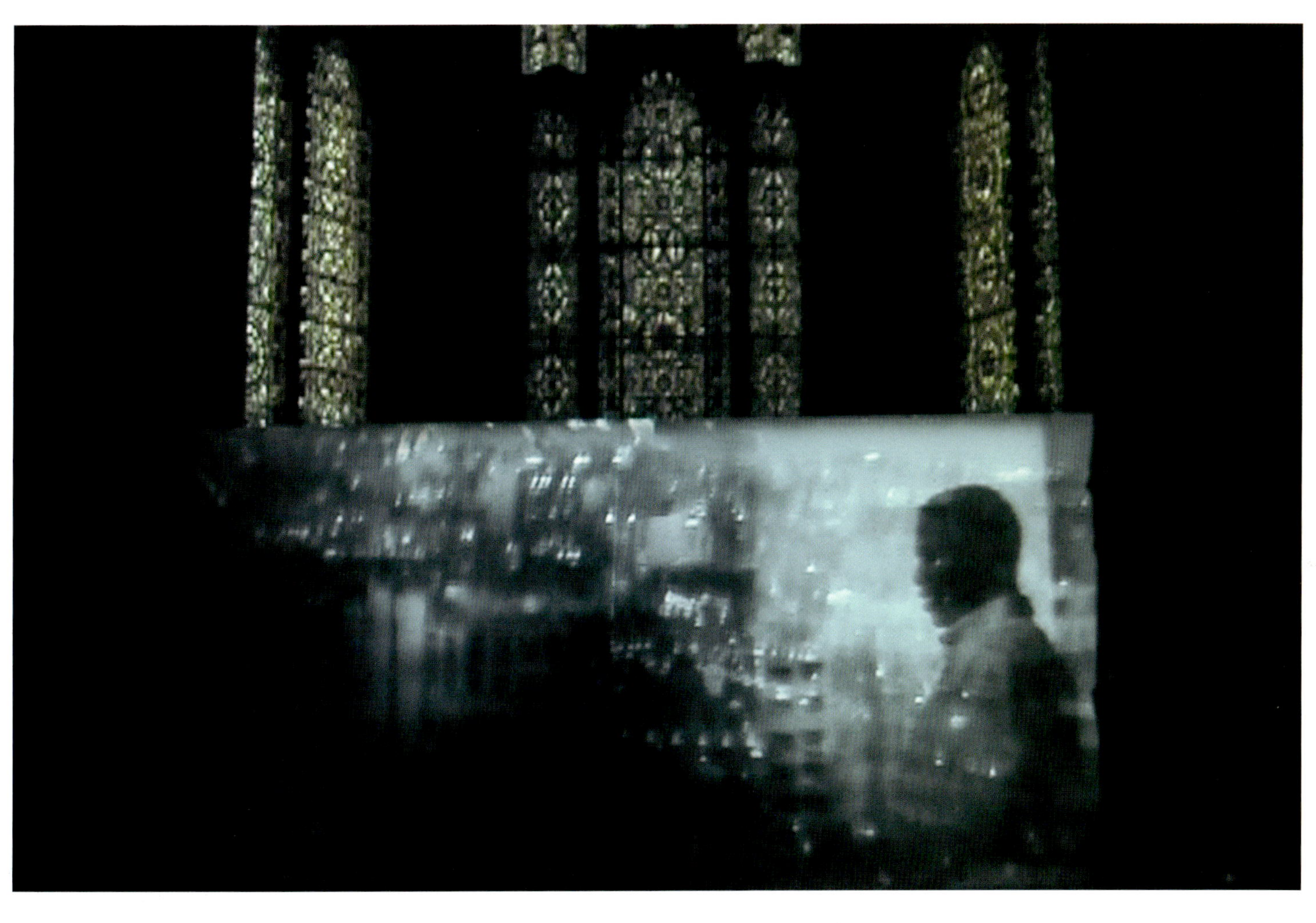

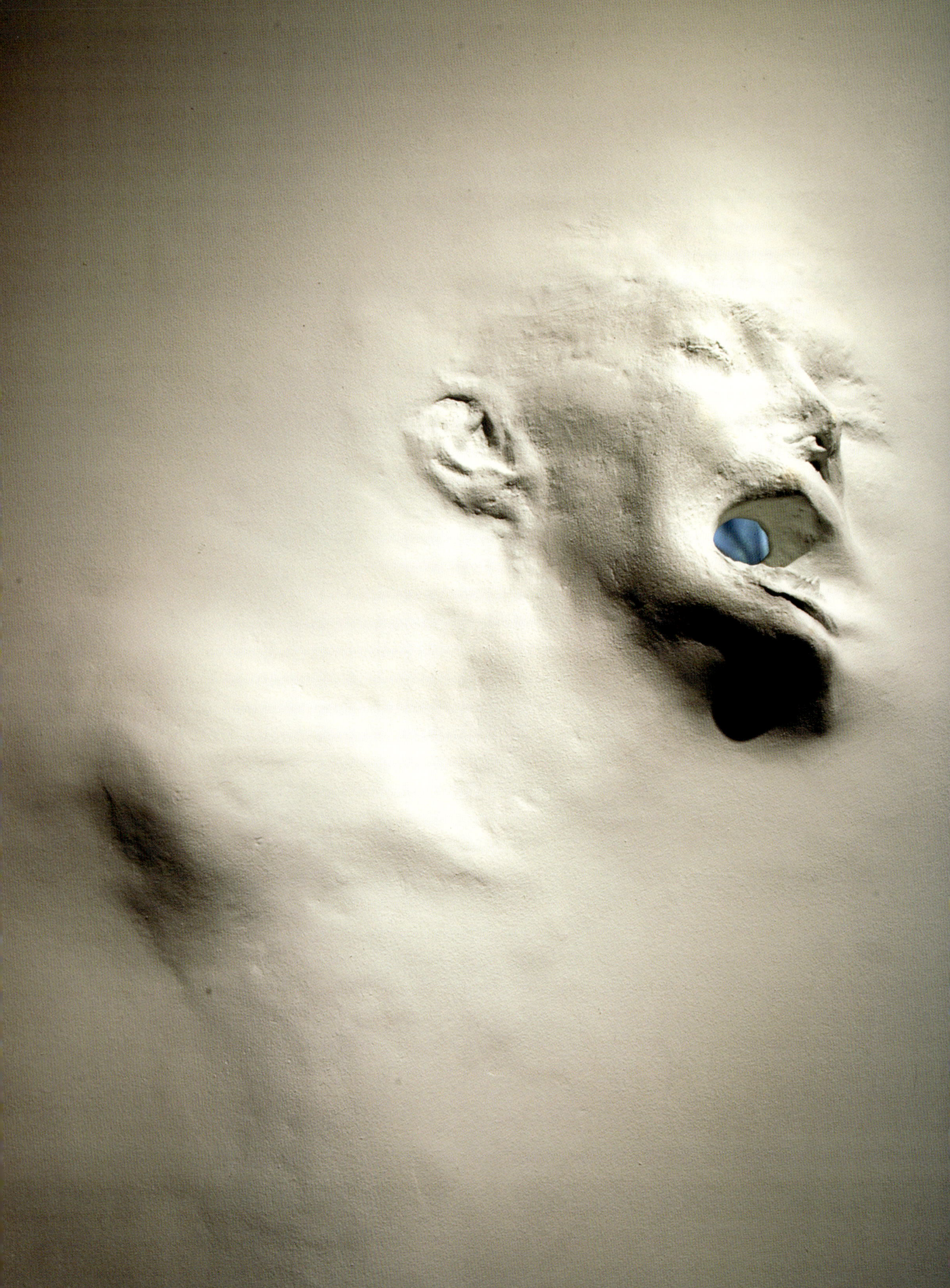

Cyclops
2004
Sculpture and DVD installation
DURATION VIDEO 2 MINS 19 SEC; AUDIO 4 MINS
Museum for African Art, 2004

Commissioned by *Season South Africa* for *Personal Affects*
Courtesy of the artist and Serge Ziegler Gallery

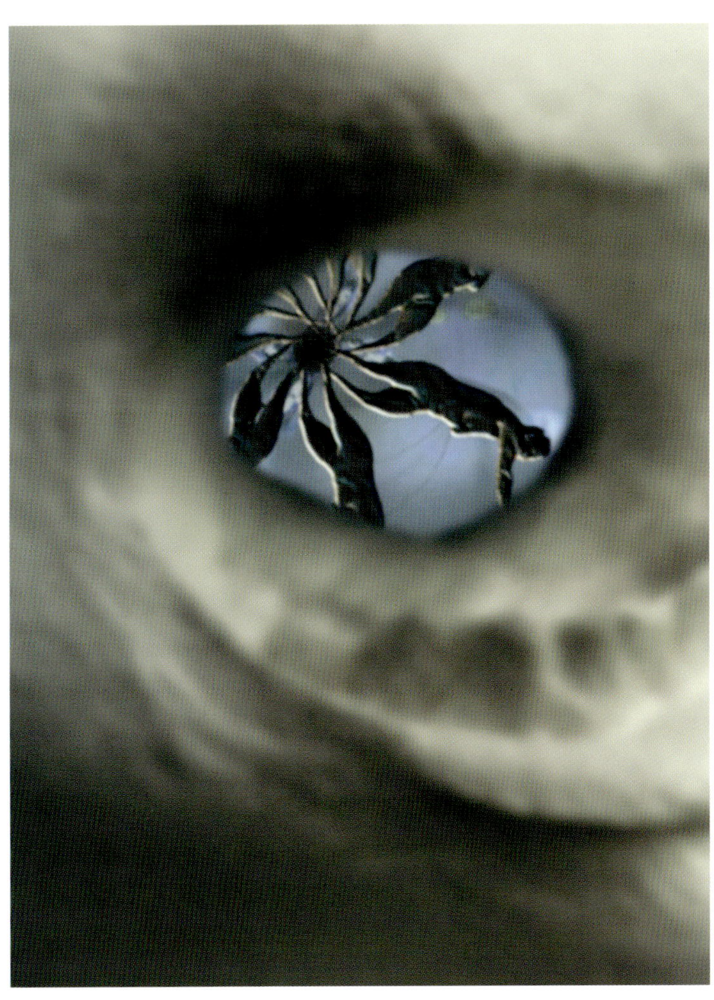

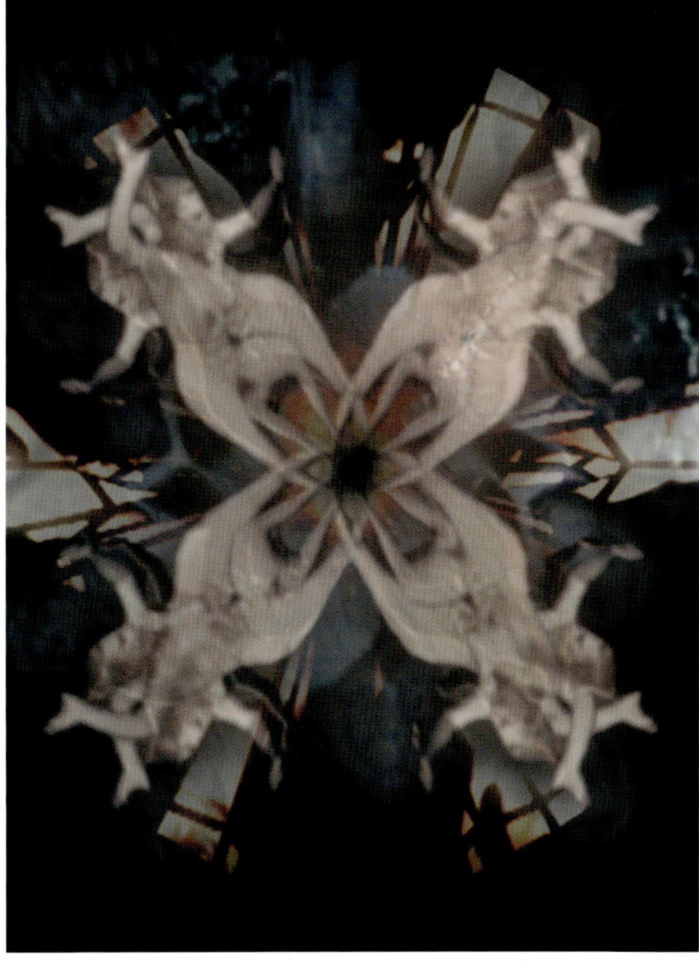

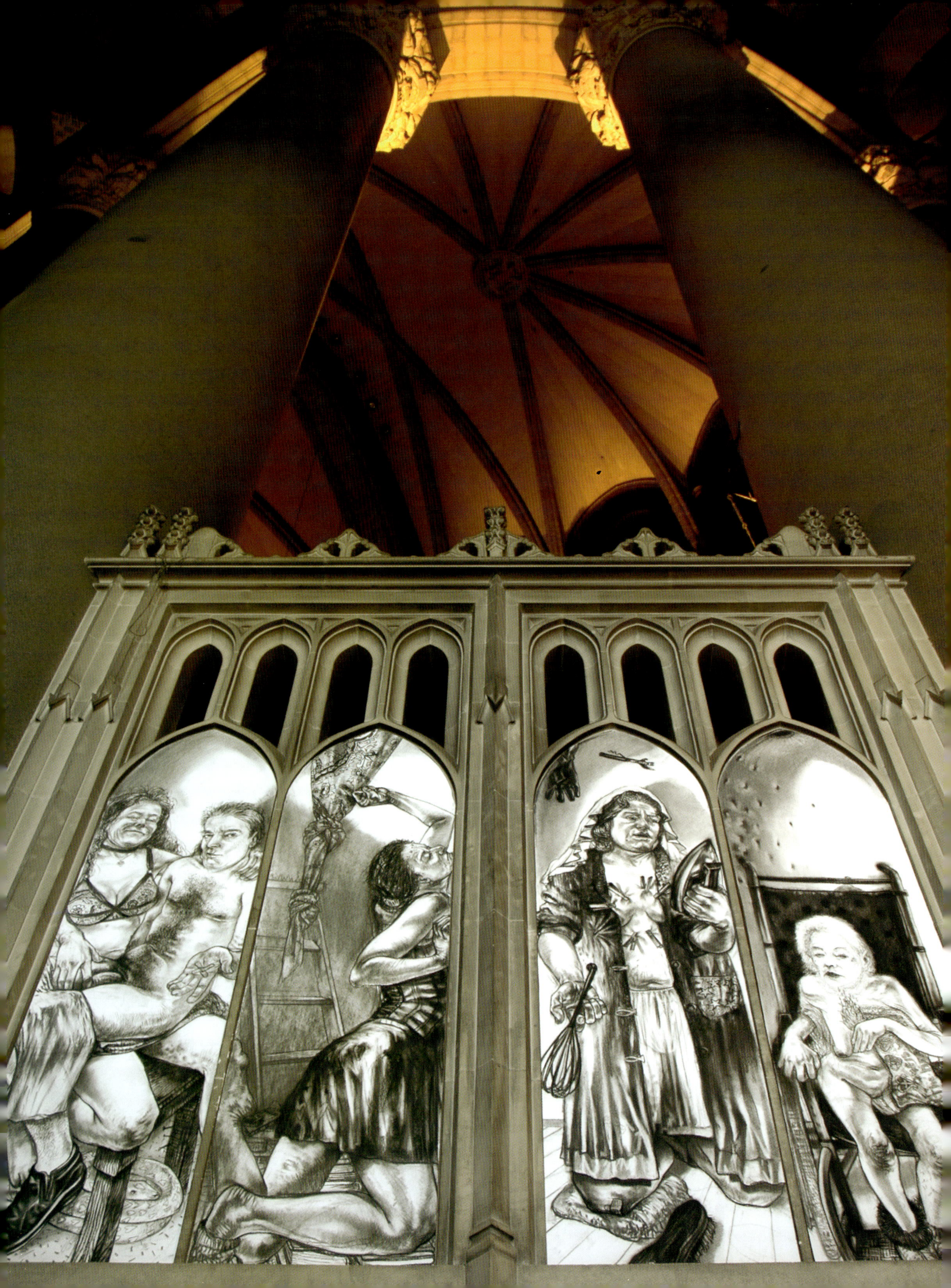

DIANE VICTOR

The Eight Mary's
2004
Charcoal on paper
EIGHT PANELS, 170 X 51 CM EACH
Opposite the Chapels of St Boniface and St Ambrose,
Cathedral of St John the Divine, 2004

Commissioned by *Season South Africa* for *Personal Affects*
Courtesy of the artist

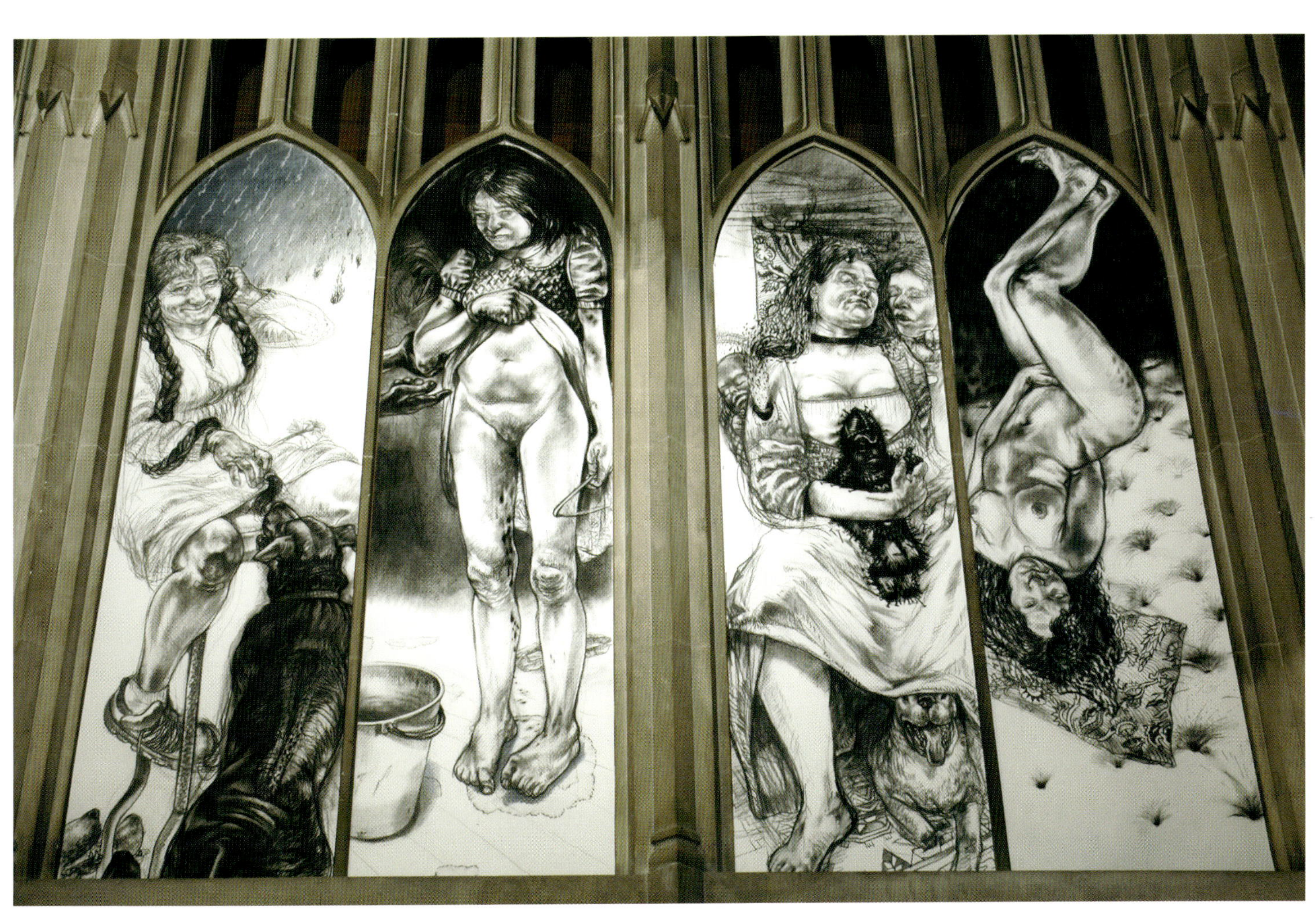

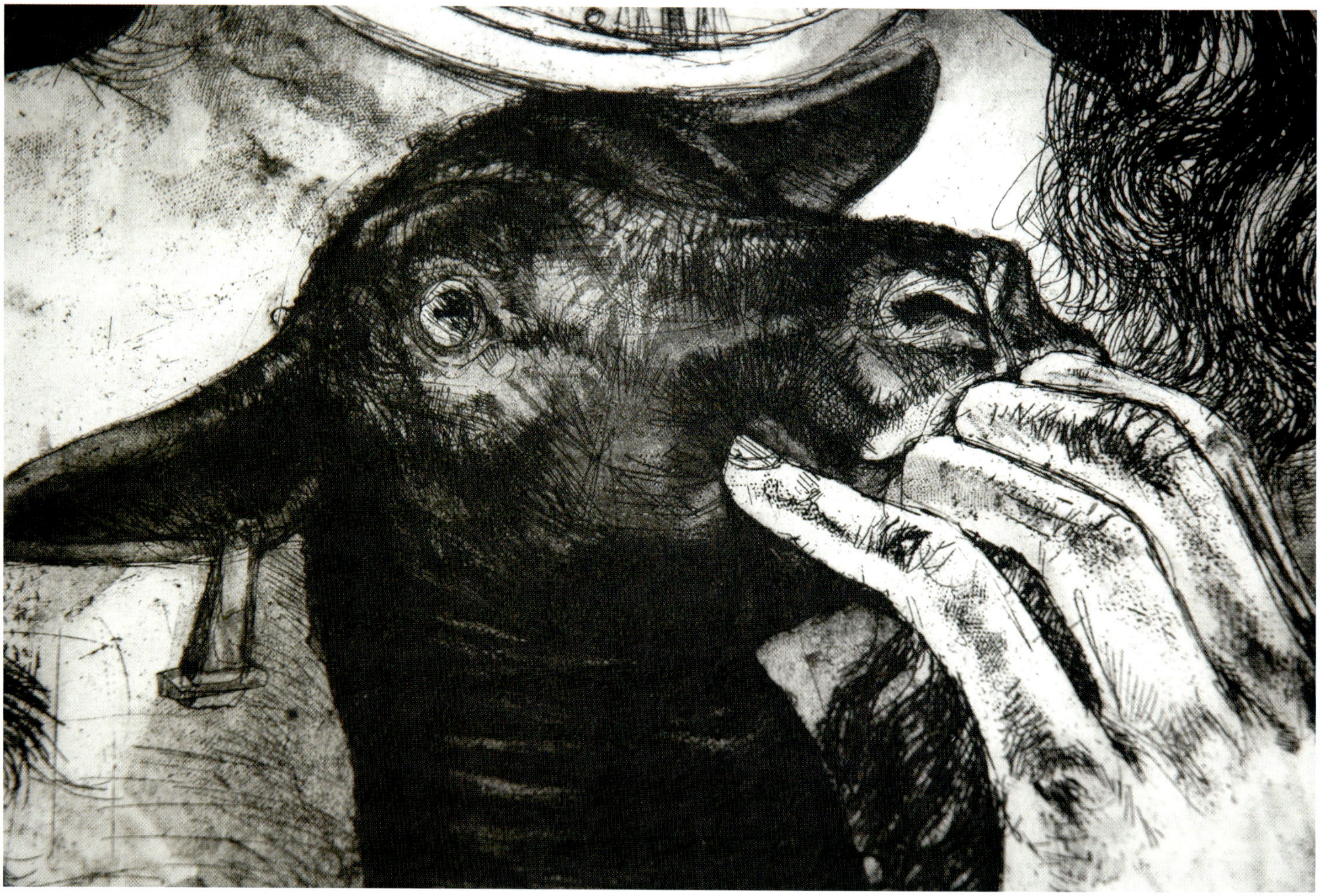

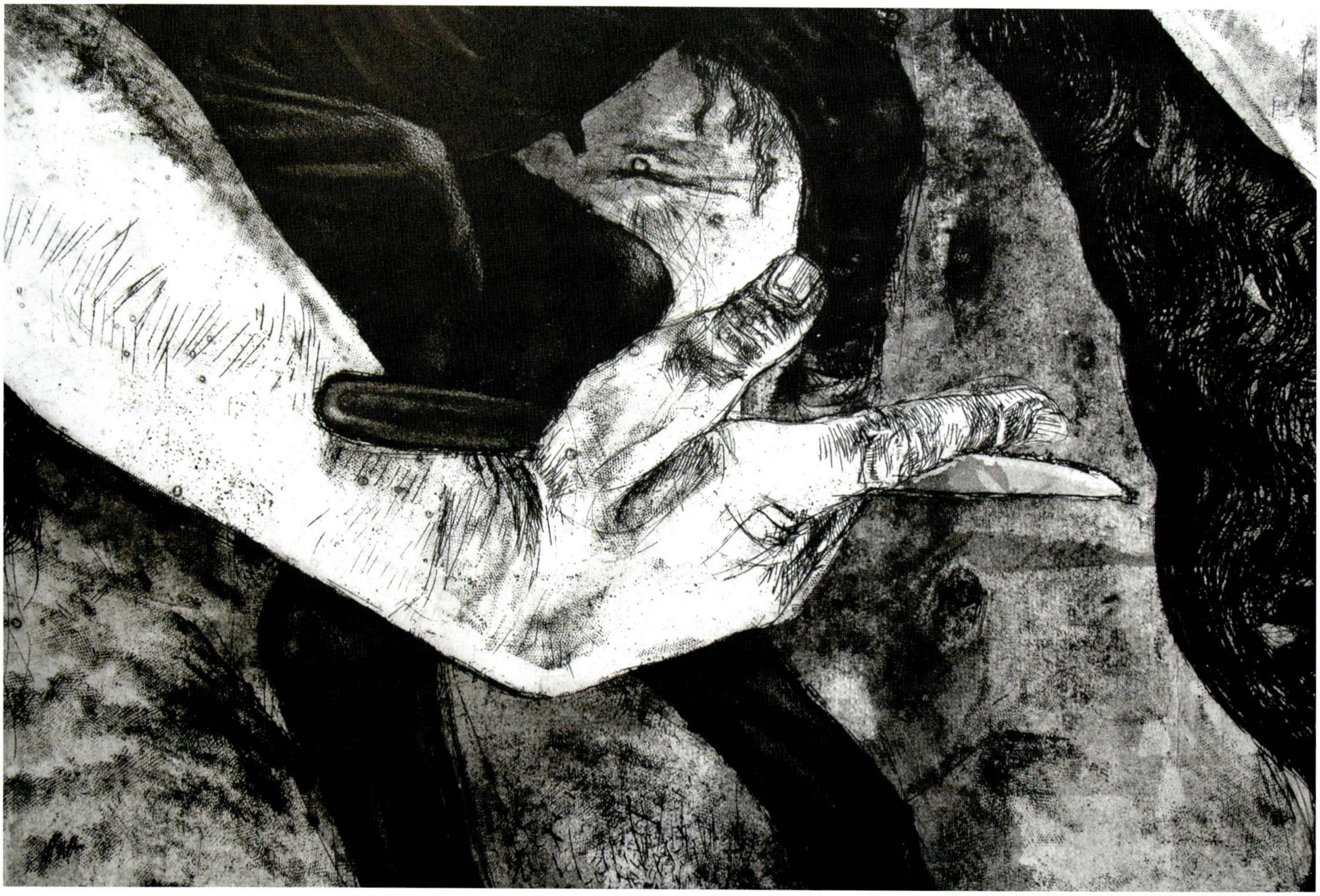

Mater, Minder, Martyr
2004
Etching, mezzotint and embossing
TRIPTYCH, 199 X 97,5 CM EACH
Museum for African Art, 2004

Commissioned by *Season South Africa* for *Personal Affects*
Courtesy of the artist

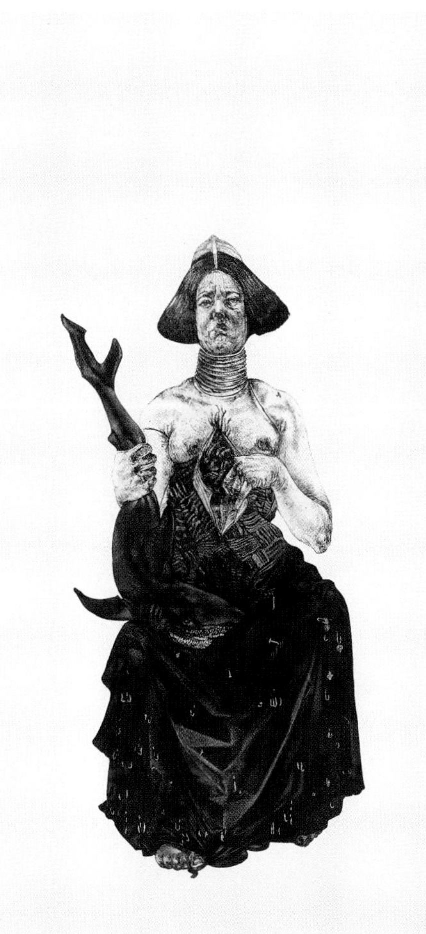

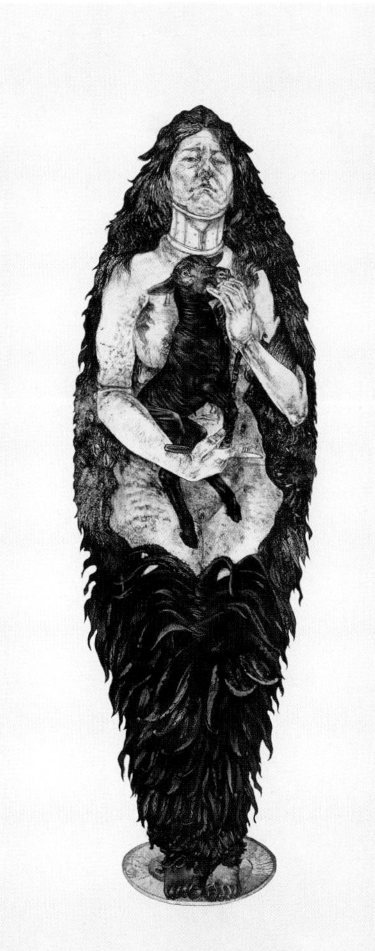

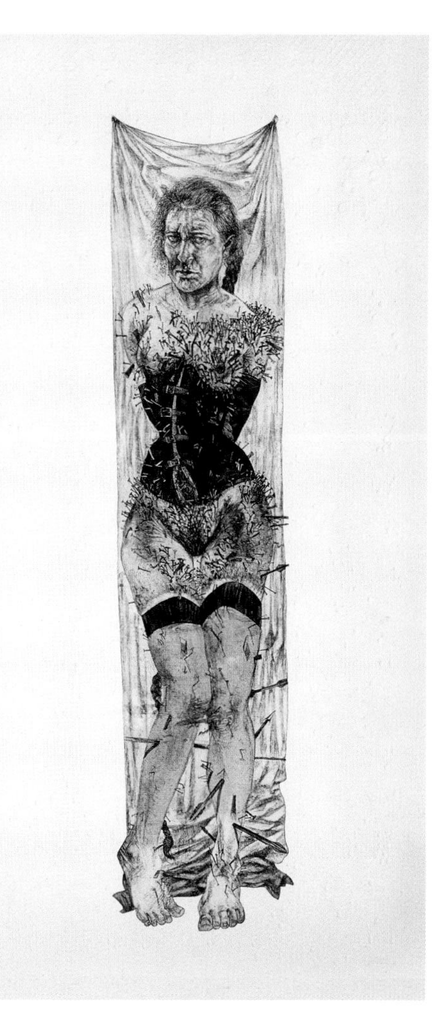

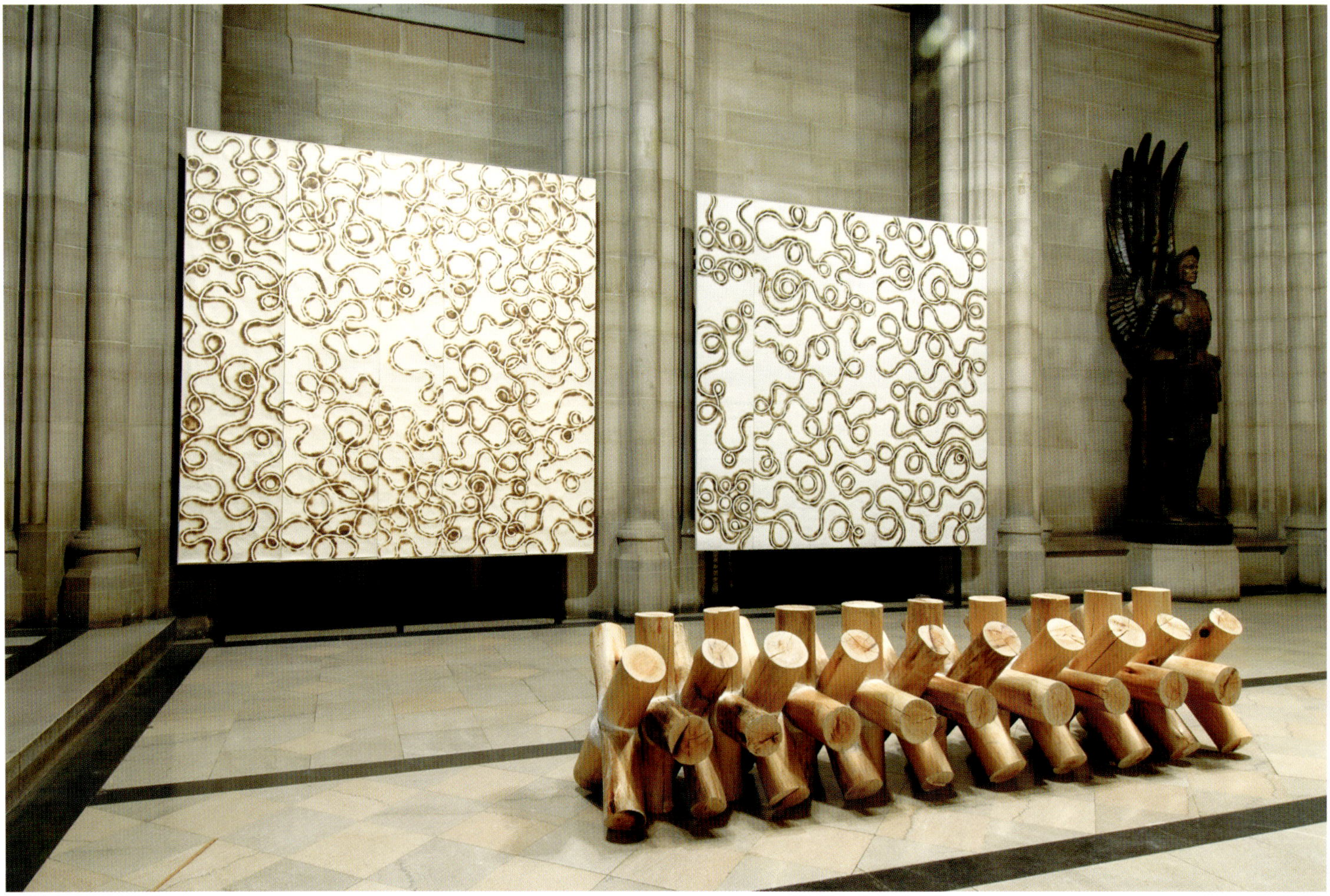

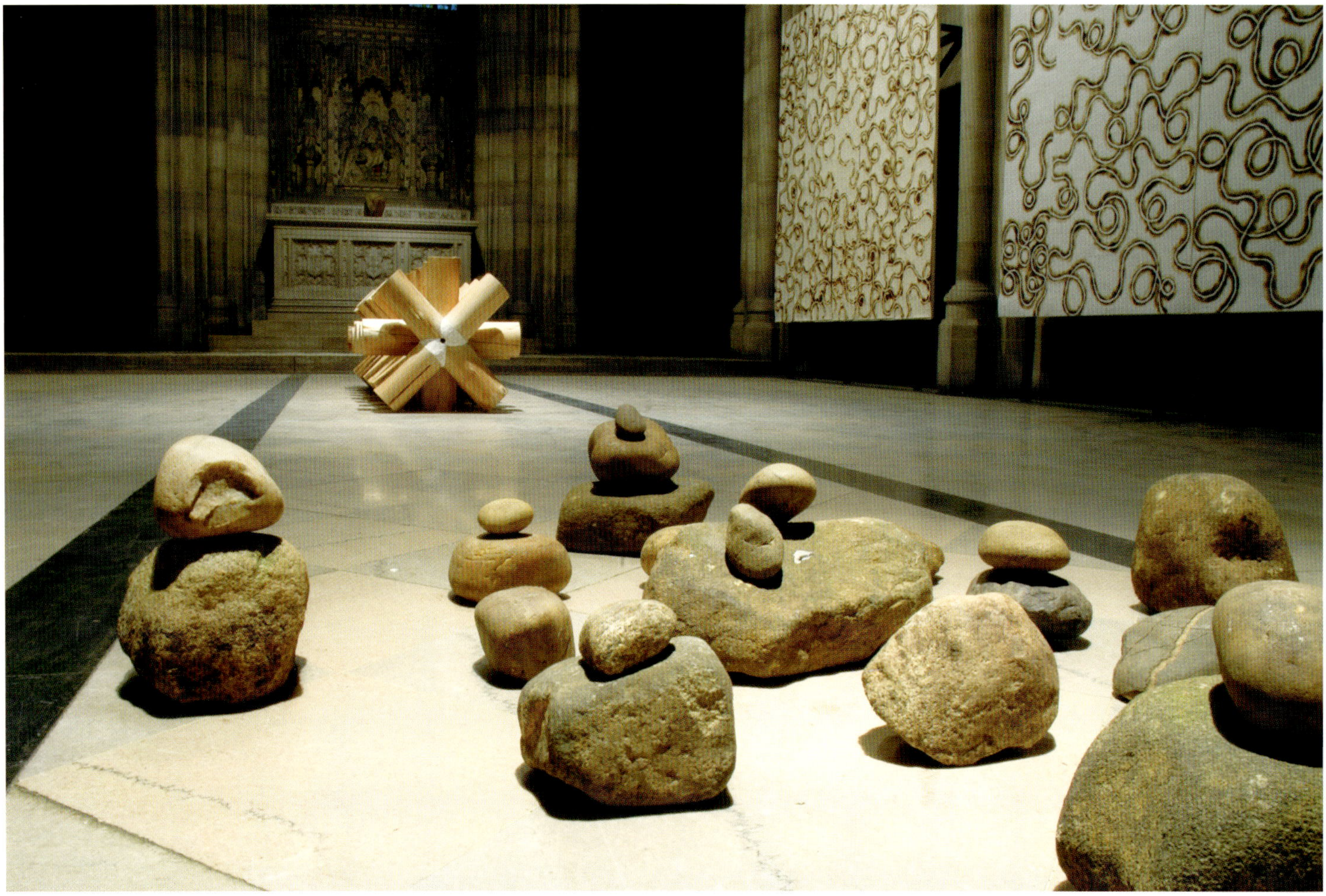

SANDILE ZULU

Spinal / Lines of Origin
2004
Mixed media including wood, stones, fire on paper
DIMENSIONS VARIABLE
Chapel of St Boniface, Cathedral of St John the Divine, 2004

Commissioned by *Season South Africa* for *Personal Affects*
Courtesy of the artist and Michael Stevenson Contemporary

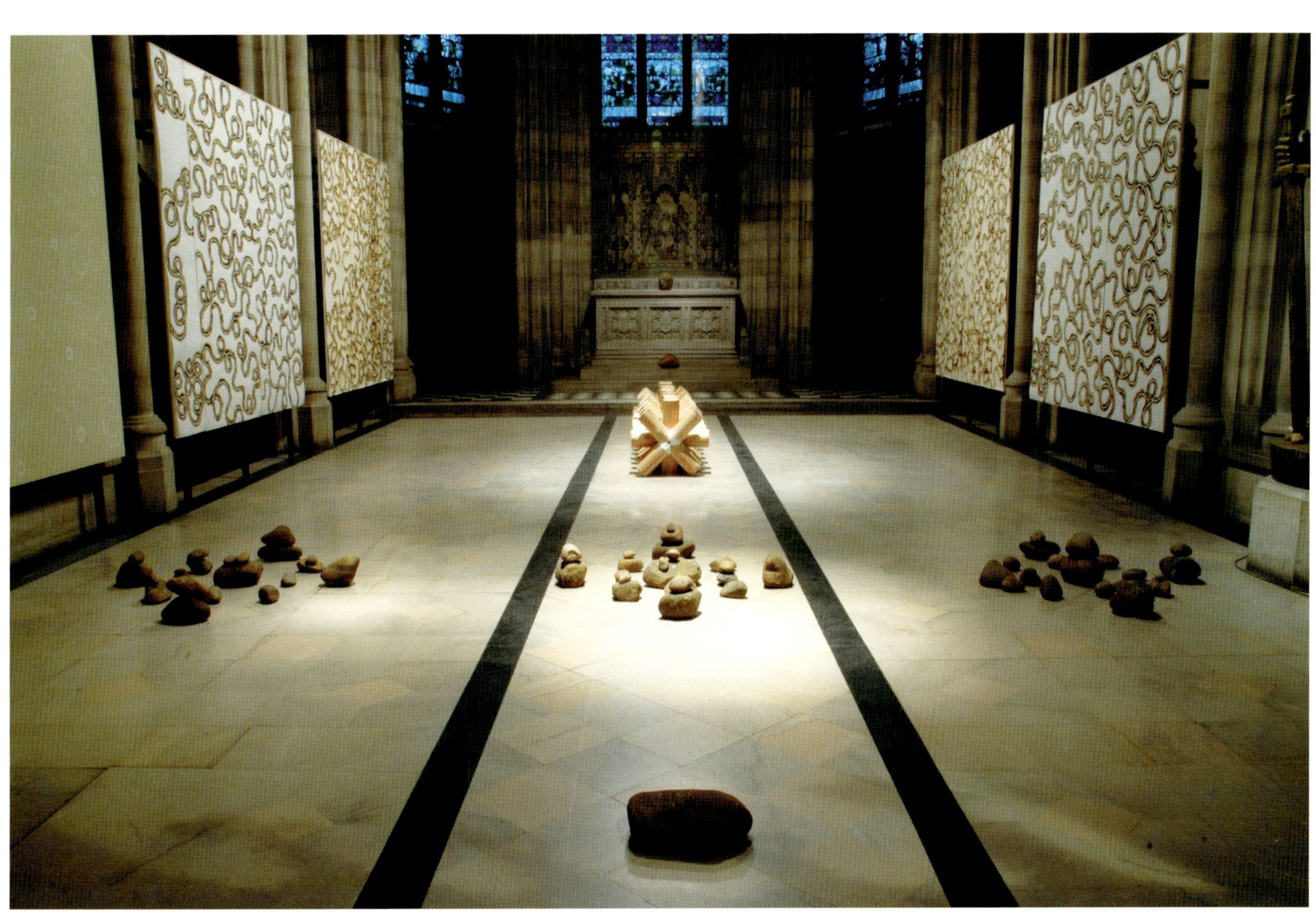

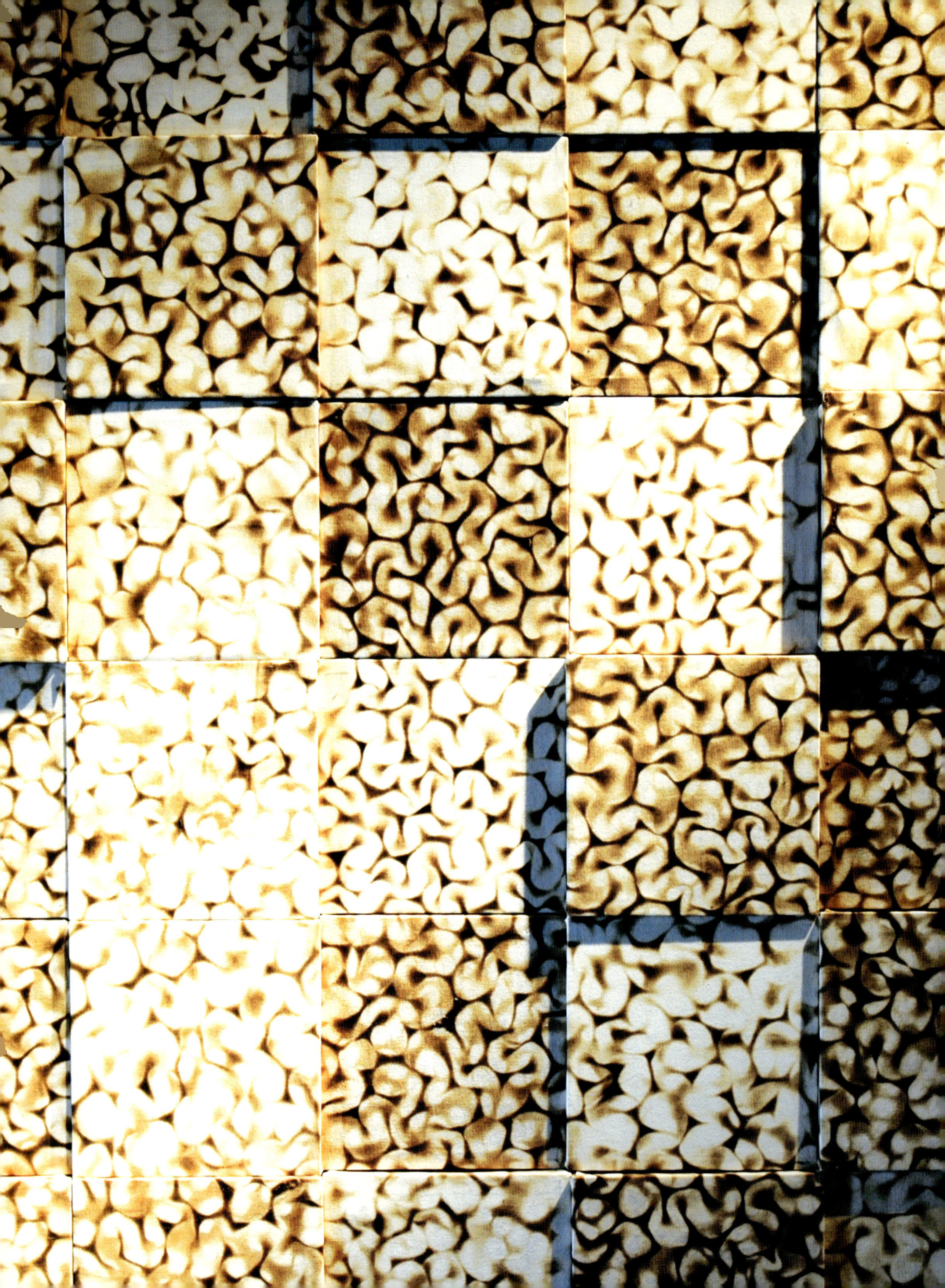

The Labyrinth of Genes and Elements III
2004
Fire, water, earth and air on canvas
273 X 163 CM
Museum for African Art, 2004

Commissioned by *Season South Africa* for *Personal Affects*
Courtesy of the artist and Michael Stevenson Contemporary

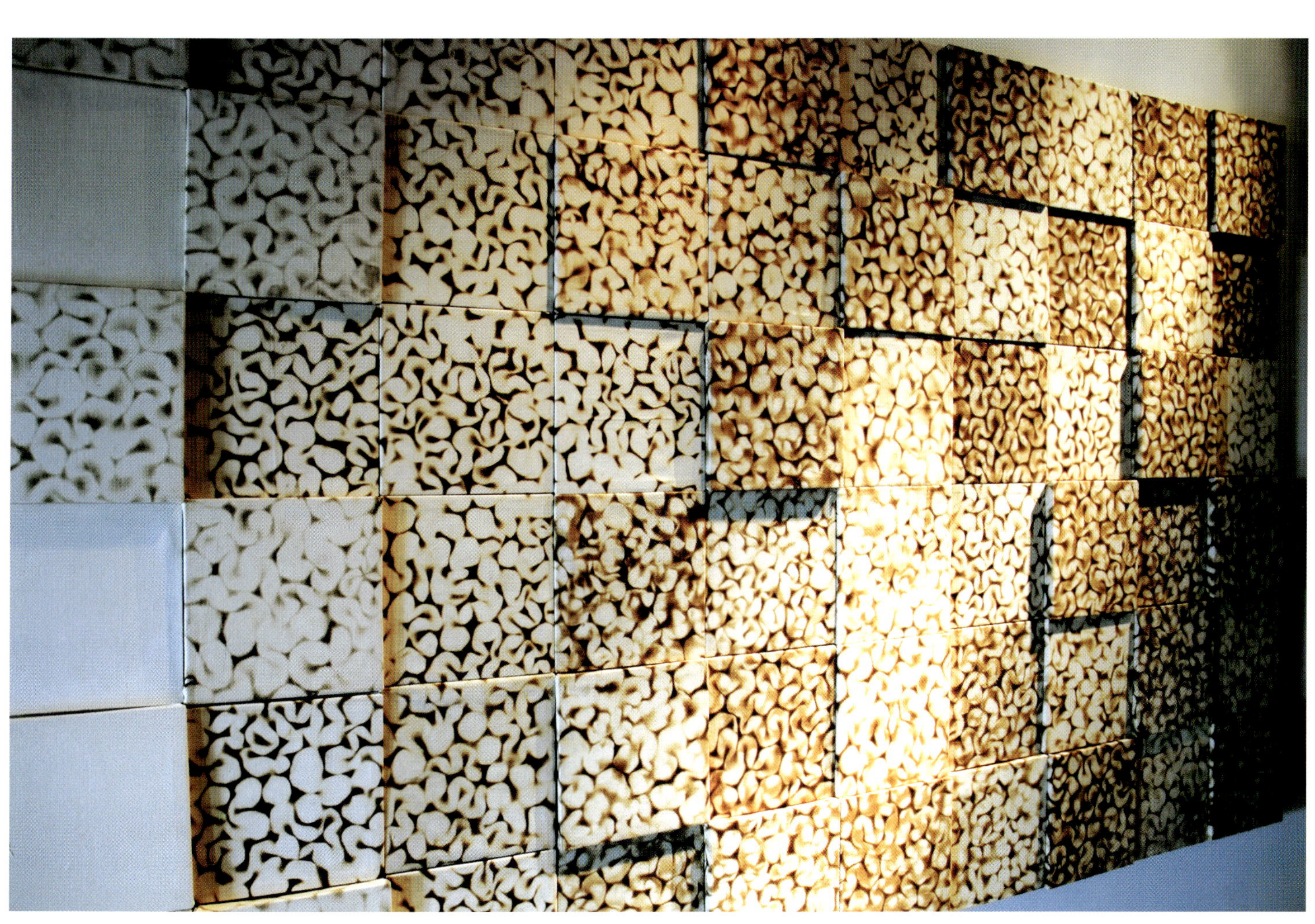

MUSEUM FOR AFRICAN ART

Foundation, Corporate & Government Donors

Altria Group, Inc.
Carnegie Corporation of New York
Community Preservation Corporation
Freshfields, Bruckhaus, Deringer LLP
Fundação Calouste Gulbenkian
Institute of Museum & Library Services
JP Morgan Chase & Co.
LEF Foundation
MasterCard International
Merrill Lynch & Co.
The Nathan Cummings Foundation, Inc.
National Endowment for the Arts
National Endowment for the Humanities
NYC Department of Cultural Affairs
The Andy Warhol Foundation for the Visual Arts

Bank of America
Con Edison
Fried, Frank, Harris, Shriver & Jacobson LLP
The GE Foundation
MasterCard International
The Mitsui USA Foundation
National Recreation Foundation
Shearman & Sterling
Tishman Realty and Construction
Toyota Motor North America, Inc.
UBS Paine Webber, Inc.

Bloomberg
Colgate-Palmolive Company
Continental Airlines
Credit Suisse First Boston
Debevoise & Plimpton
Deloitte & Touche
The Irene Diamond Fund
Entrust Capital, Inc.
Étant donnés: The French-American Fund for
  Contemporary Art
Goldman, Sachs & Co.
HSBC Bank USA
KeySpan Foundation
l'AFFA/Programme Afrique en creations
Mondriaan Foundation
Movado Group
New York State Council on the Arts
The New York Times Company Foundation
Oppenheimer & Co.
May and Samuel Rudin Family Foundation
United Way of New York City
Verizon
Washington Mutual Bank

American Express Company
Citigroup Private Bank
Cushman & Wakefield
The Irene Diamond Fund
Marsh USA Inc.
Marsh & McLennan Companies Inc.
Newmont Mining Corporation
New School University
New York Council for the Humanities
The New Yorker
NTT America, Inc.
Pfizer Inc.
Ricoh Corporation
Schieffelin & Somerset
Seedco
Time Incorporated
Time Warner
U.S. News & World Report
The Wall Street Journal
The Walt Disney Company
Xerox Corporation

Ambac Financial Group, Inc.
Fundação Luso-Americana
Tonio Burgos & Associates

Individual Donors

Corice Canton Arman and Arman
Mr. Henry Buhl
Ms. Marion Green
Jane and Gerald Katcher
Kathryn McAuliffe and Jay Kriegel
Mrs. Cecilia Smiley
Jerome and Ellen Stern
Mr. John Tishman
Mr. Jason H. Wright

Mr. and Mrs. Charles B. Benenson
Mr. Lawrence Benenson
Mr. Ed Bradley and Ms. Patricia Blanchet
Martin and Shirley Bresler
Mr. Bruce Brickman
Dr. and Mrs. Sidney Clyman
Mr. Jonathan D. Green
Mr. Irwin Ginsburg
Mr. Lawrence Gussman
Mr. Hans Hageman
Ms. Kimberly Hardy
Dr. Sidney Hart
Ms. Jane B. Holzer
Ms. Patricia Irvin, Esq.
Helen and Martin Kimmel
Mrs. Jo Levitt
Dr. Andreas Lindner
Drs. Marian and Daniel Malcolm
Jennifer and Art Mbanefo
Ms. Veronica Pollard
Mr. Onuoha Odim
Mr. and Mrs. James J. Ross
Lynne and Robert Rubin
Daniel Shapiro and Agnes Gund
Mr. Dennis Swanson

Ms. Joan Barist
Mr. and Mrs. Carlo Bella
Diana and Richard Beattie
Mr. and Mrs. Kojo Bentil
Linda and Bruce Bodner
Mr. and Mrs. Woodrow Campbell
Mr. and Mrs. Louis Capozzi
Ms. Gwen L. Carr
John W. Carr, Esq.
Ms. Diahann Carroll
Mr. David Christensen
Dorothy and Lewis Cullman
Mr. Samuel S. Daniel
Mr. Charles Davis
Kurt and Mary Delbanco
Lee Dunham
Drs. Jean and Noble Endicott
Mr. Lance Entwistle
Dr. and Mrs. Aaron Esman
Michael and Nancy Feller
Ms. Vianna Finch
Ms. Jane Fincher
Jacques and Nathalie Germain
Denyse and Marc Ginzberg
Mr. David Goldring
Mr. and Mrs. Stephen Goldstone
Mr. James Gorman
Mr. Jonathan D. Green
Myrna and Stephen Greenberg
Ms. Gail Gregg and Mr. Arthur Sulzberger
Lesley and Evan Heller
Mr. and Mrs. John Herrmann
Mr. Derek Q. Johnson
Mr. LLoyd Kaplan
Ms. Zelda Kaplan
Mr. and Mrs. Peter Klosowicz
Mr. and Mrs. Arthur Kramer
Mr. and Mrs. Jay Last
Caral and Joe Lebworth
Mrs. Dorothy Lichtenstein
Mr. Adam Lindemann
Mr. Vincent Mai
Ms. Marian Marill
Ms. Elsie McCabe

Jeanne Moutoussamy-Ashe
Mr. and Mrs. Daniel Murnick
Amyas Naegle
Mr. Robert Neimeth
Mr. and Mrs. Richard Parsons
Mr. and Mrs. Peter O. Price
Mr. David Rockefeller
Beatrice Riese
Holly and David Ross
Mrs. Harry Rubin
Mr. Bruce Saber
Mr. Ralph Schlosstein
Dr. and Mrs. Morton Schwimmer
Mr. and Mrs. Maurice Solomon
Mr. Jeff Soref
The Honorable Percy C. Sutton
Julie Taymor
Mr. Jonathan M. Tisch
Mr. Bernard Tschumi
Ms. Helen Tucker
Mr. Kevin Umeh
Ms. Ellen Urell
Mr. Jerome Vogel
Ms. Claudia Wagner
Mr. Robert T. Wall
Mr. Tom Wesselmann
Janice Savin Williams and Christopher J.
  Williams
Ms. Elease Wright
Harold and Maureen Zarember
Mr. Daniel Ziff
Mr. Al Zollar

Anonymous
Mr. and Mrs. Roger Altman
Ms. Lillian Barrios-Paoli
Mrs. Patti Cadby Birch
Mr. and Mrs. Daniel L. Black
Ronald and Linda Blatt
Ms. Betty Bobrow
Ms. Janis Gardner Cecil
Christo and Jeanne Claude
Mrs. Katherine Cline
Dr. and Mrs. Oliver E. Cobb
Ms. Martha Cotter and Mr. Alan Sussman
Mr. and Mrs. Thomas D'Agostino
Ms. Gail Yvette Davis
Ms. Barbaralee Diamonstein and Mr. Carl Spielvogel
The Honorable David N. Dinkins
James R. and Nina H. Donnelley
Ms. Susan Fales-Hill
Mr. Richard Faletti
Mr. Bill Hodges
Mr. and Mrs. Carroll Janis
Ellen Kaplowitz
Mr. Luciano Lanfranchi
Guy and Roxanne Lanquetot
Leonard and Evelyn Lauder
Diane and Brian Leyden
Mr. Robin Magowan and Ms. Juliet Mattila
Mr. Peter Marino
Mr. Raymond J. McGuire
Ms. Bella Meyer
Mr. Steven Morris
Mr. Harvey S. Shipley Miller
Mrs. Kendall A. Mix
Ms. Maria Patterson
Mr. and Mrs. Sammy Ofer
Mr. and Mrs. Fred M. Richman
Mr. and Mrs. Richard Rothman
Ms. Elizabeth Seidman
Ms. Carolyn Setlow
Ms. Ruth Lande Shuman
Merton D. Simpson
Ms. Lowery Stokes Sims
Ms. Victoria Lea Smith
Ann and Paul Sperry
Mr. and Mrs. Toshiaki Taguchi
Mr. Lucien Van de Velde
Ms. Kathy van der Pas
Mr. William Van Parys
Ms. Adrienne Vittadini
Mr. and Mrs. George Wein
Dr. Frederick B. Williams
Mr. and Mrs. Lester Wunderman

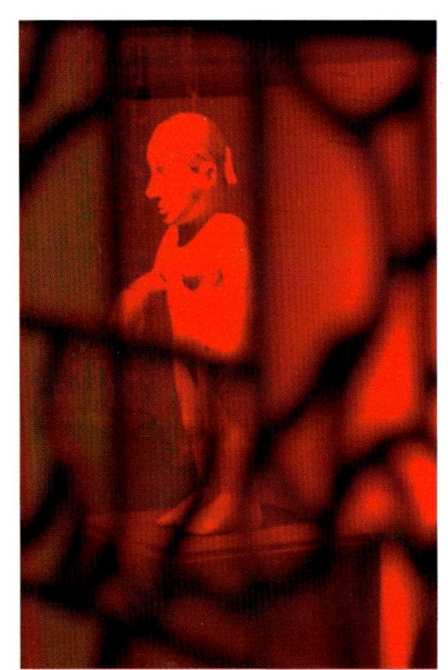